Collins

DigiTech 3

Manasi Kashikar
Sneha Krishnan

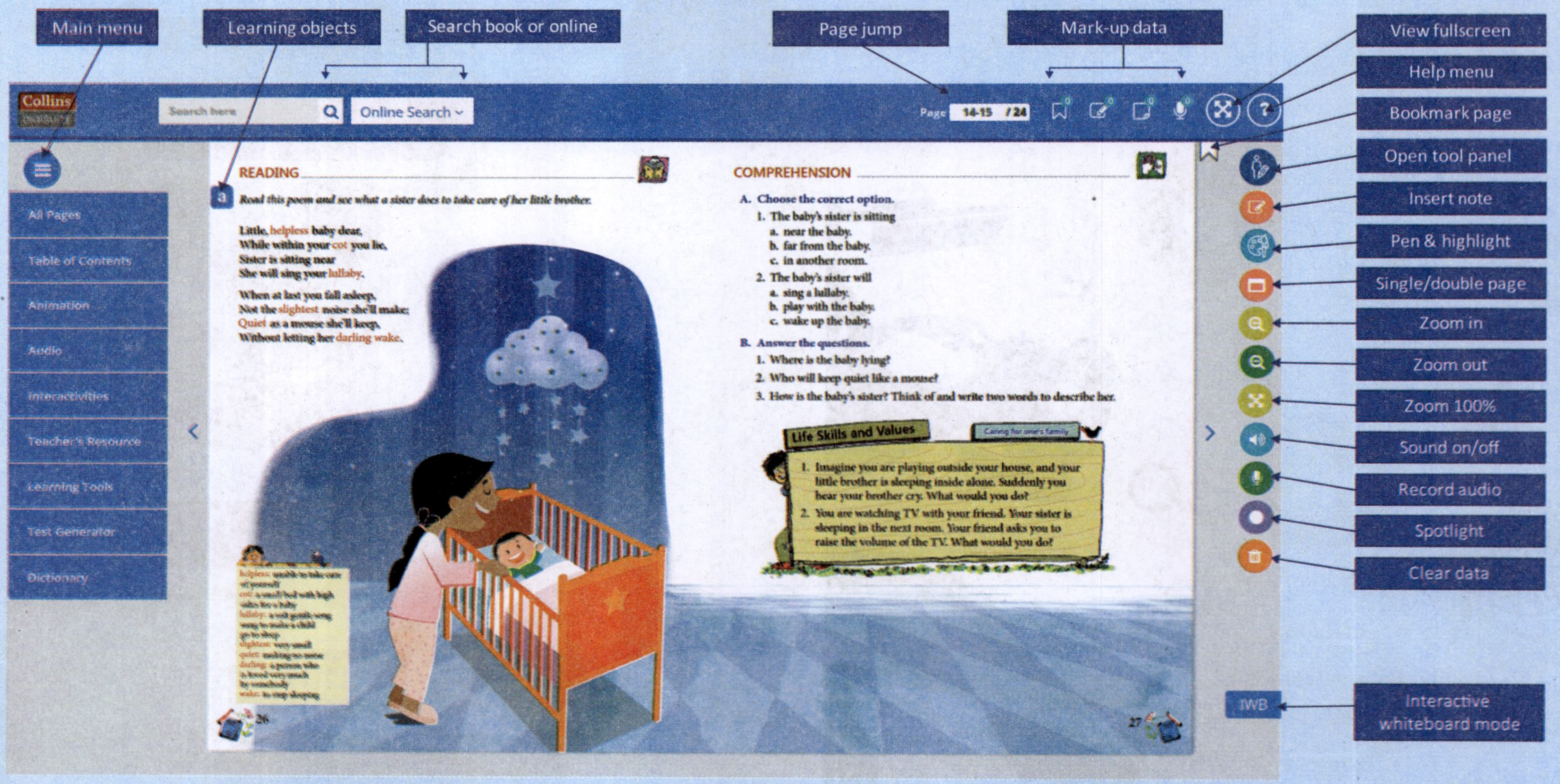

Student + Teacher			Teacher-only	
a animations	**ia** activities	**g** games	**lp** lesson plans	**tn** teacher's notes
ilt instructor-led tutorials	**w** worksheets	**v** videos	**w** worksheets	**ak** answer keys
	audio			

PREFACE

Over the last few decades, technology has touched almost all aspects of our lives. As technology continues to evolve more rapidly than ever, users are learning newer ways of harnessing the power of technology in their daily lives. In India, easy access to smartphones and affordable internet services have put the power of technology in the hands of millions.

In this backdrop, we believe, it is important for students to:

- ✓ Understand that technology is going to keep evolving. As citizens of the digital world that we all inhabit, keeping abreast of the latest advances is no longer optional, rather, it is an essential life skill.
- ✓ Appreciate that coding skills are as essential today as basic literacy and numeracy. This has been emphasized in the National Educational Policy of 2020 as well.
- ✓ Understand that technology is pervasive and they need to be able to comprehend its intersection with other disciplines. In other words, they need to learn to use technology as a tool to achieve a goal.
- ✓ Take control of regulating their usage and make constructive use of their access to computer devices.

While authoring this series, we have designed and presented the content with the intent of helping students in developing the skills described above. We have ensured that the topics are covered in a relatable manner and that the exercises are practical and applicable. The textbook along with its resources for teachers will enable them to deliver this subject effectively, while keeping the students engaged and interested.

In addition to the curriculum imperatives, we have included concepts as outlined in the National Education Policy 2020. Every grade has computational thinking–based practice problems that are aligned to Bloom's Taxonomy. Topics such as coding and app development have been given their due consideration as their relevance increases in the real world and while making career choices. Artificial intelligence has been woven into the chapters in an age-appropriate manner in the form of Fun with AI boxes, with the intent of enabling students to understand key concepts and applications of AI.

The series equips students with not only the skills required to excel in technology and make the most of it, but also exposes them to the practical applications of these in the world around them.

We would like to thank our intern Sejal Gupta in helping us shape the content.

KEY FEATURES

After reading this chapter, I will be able to:

- ✔ Describe a computer system.
- ✔ Describe the IPO cycle.
- ✔ Describe the meaning and use of hardware and software.
- ✔ Describe the components of the CPU.

Well-defined learning objectives that are mapped to the curriculum to help students identify the topics they will read about in the chapter

Activities and discussions based on real-life situations to set the context for what students are about to lear

Cross Curricular

Brainstorm and explore!

Zoya and Jatin have gone for a picnic with their parents. Look at the given picture and answer the following questions.

Soak up!

The first six letters in the first row of the letter keys are Q, W, E, R, T and Y. Thus, this keyboard is called the QWERTY keyboard.

Additional information/facts about the topic being taught

Contextual meaning of difficult words

As the name suggests, the user interface enables the user to interact with the computer. A graphical user interface uses visual elements, such as images and icons to enable the user to interact with the computer.

interface: common point between two things to ensure smooth working between them

Technology Literacy

Crank up!

The command line feature can be accessed on Windows devices with the help of the command prompt. To access it, type 'cmd' in the Search bar.

Tips and shortcut tricks for the topics covered in the chapter to foster inquiry- and discovery-based learning

Clear up!

Just like changing the desktop background, can you change the colour of the taskbar using the Colors option in the Personalize window?

Hands-on tasks for revision, based on the application of the concept taught

Brush up!

Discuss with your teacher and classmates about software. Write names of some application and system software.

System software: ______________________________

Application software: ______________________________

Short questions to reinforce the concept learnt and promote competency-based learning

Exemplifies the relevance and application of AI to the concept in the real world

Fun with AI

Artificial Intelligence is more of a software computer program rather than hardware. To run complex AI programs, computers use special hardware, such as graphics processor unit (GPU) and more advanced CPUs. These devices enable computers to run these programs more efficiently and quickly.

Real-world examples and situations to help students establish linkages and connections to support the development of lateral thinking

Link up!

While playing games or using MS Paint, we give input to the computer by either moving the mouse or typing on the keyboard. After processing in the CPU, we get the output of the game or the drawing. All this is done in less than a second!

Recapitulates all the important points covered in the chapter

Today I learnt!

- We should always store all the data in a computer neatly, using files and folders, so that they are easy to find later.
- A file stores data and information, while a folder organizes the files in a group.
- A folder is a container to store many files.
- The File Explorer shows us drives on our computer.
- There are multiple ways of creating a file or folder on a Windows 10 computer.
- There are two ways to close a file/folder.
- We can open an already saved file or folder by simple double-clicking on its icon.

Revision exercises comprising a blend of both objective and long-answer questions, including both fact- and application-based questions in a variety of formats

Revise and polish!

Learning Skills

1. Tick (✓) the correct answer.
   a. How many scroll bars are there in a Microsoft Word 2016 document?
      (i) One ☐ (ii) Two ☐ (iii) Three ☐ (iv) Four ☐
   b. ________ is the shortcut to save a document.
      (i) Ctrl+S ☐ (ii) Ctrl+D ☐ (iii) Ctrl+P ☐ (iv) Ctrl+E ☐

Based on the practical application of the concepts taught to enhance comprehension and provide opportunities for peer tutoring

Lab Activities

Experiential Learning

Check the various hardware devices on the computer and see if you can touch all of them. Similarly, check the software programs on the computer and list down which ones are application software.

Practical applications of the concepts covered to help analyse and understand real-world situations, with some extra effort put into research and information gathering

Projects

Find out about three endangered species of animals. Gather the following information about each:

1. What is their natural habitat? Where are they found?
2. What do they eat–herbivorous, carnivorous or omnivorous.
3. Search for the pictures of male and female animals. Do they live in groups?
4. Why are they becoming extinct?
5. What can we do to prevent their extinction?

Use this information to put together a presentation. Format the presentation so that it looks bright and colourful.

Worksheet 2 (Chapters 3 and 4)

Learning Skills

1. Draw the symbols used to represent the following tabs/tools.
   a. Cut ☐ b. Undo ☐ c. Web browser of your choice ☐

Chapter-based revision worksheets focused on competency-based learning and one dedicated worksheet on developing computational thinking through playing games and problem-solving

NEP IN DIGI TECH

These are some of the key skills that you will see occurring throughout the books at various stages.

21st Century Skills

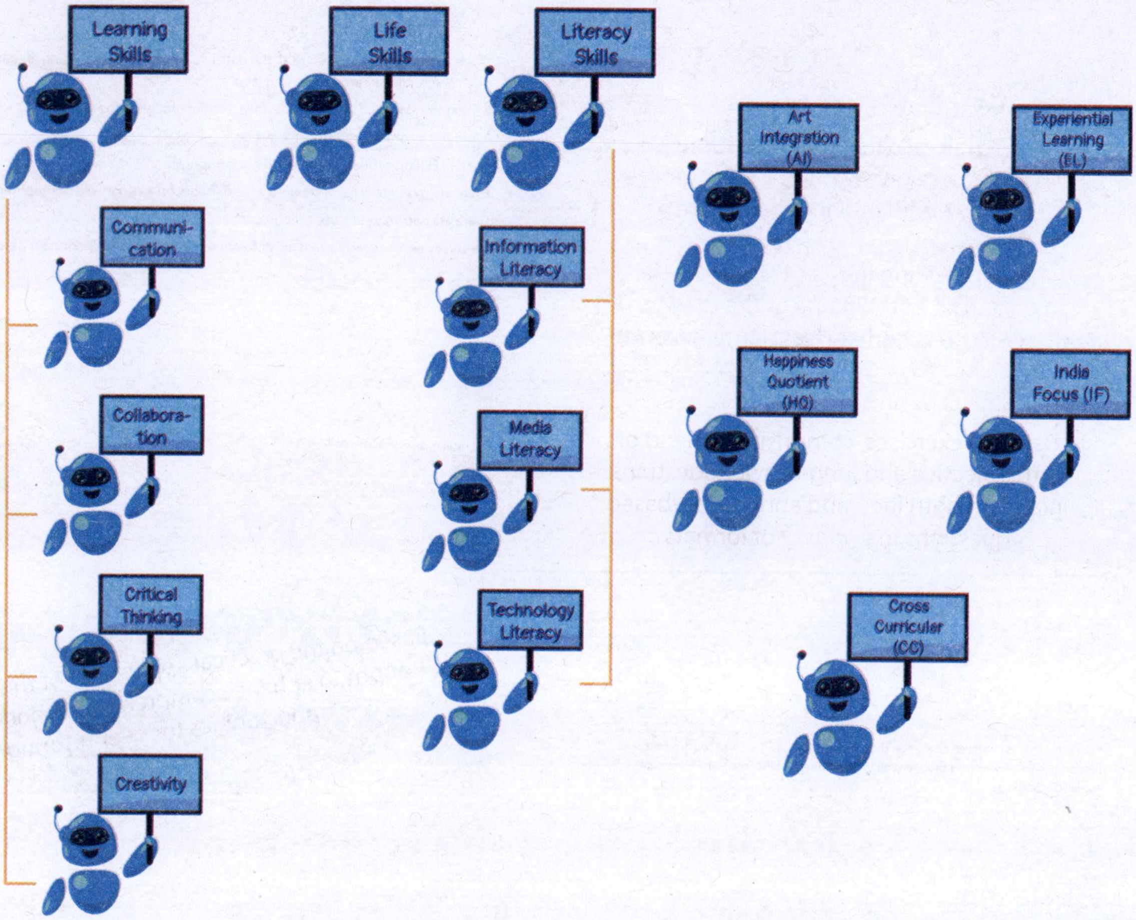

ABOUT THE AUTHORS

Sneha Krishnan and **Manasi Kashikar**, techies at heart, bond over their love of coding. They are co-founders of the company *MindChamp* where they teach coding to school students using fun, activity-based learning. They both love to teach students and that reflects in their work. Together with a team of educators, they have taught thousands of students to create computer games and websites. They want to make coding accessible to young students as well, so they are better equipped for the future.

CONTENTS

Chapter 1

A Computer System

After reading this chapter, I will be able to:

- ✔ Describe a computer system.
- ✔ Describe the meaning and use of hardware and software.
- ✔ Describe the IPO cycle.
- ✔ Describe the components of the CPU.

Brainstorm and explore!

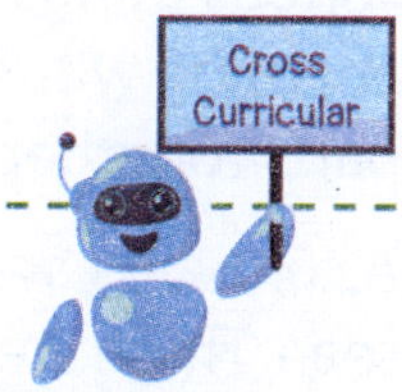

The five sense organs of the body are: eyes, ears, nose, tongue and skin. They help us in doing different activities. For example, our eyes and ears help us to be aware of things around us.

Can you identify these organs as input/output parts? Tick (✔) the parts that work as an input part for our body and cross (✘) the parts that work as an output part for our body. Circle the part if it can be used both for input and output.

We know that a computer is a machine. It can be used to perform different kinds of tasks. Computers are very common and are used almost everywhere. Here are some of the uses of a computer:

- Schools use computers to store information about their students, teachers and exam timetables.
- Railway stations and airports use computers to track all trains and airplanes.
- At home, computers are used to play games, listen to music, watch movies and search for information.

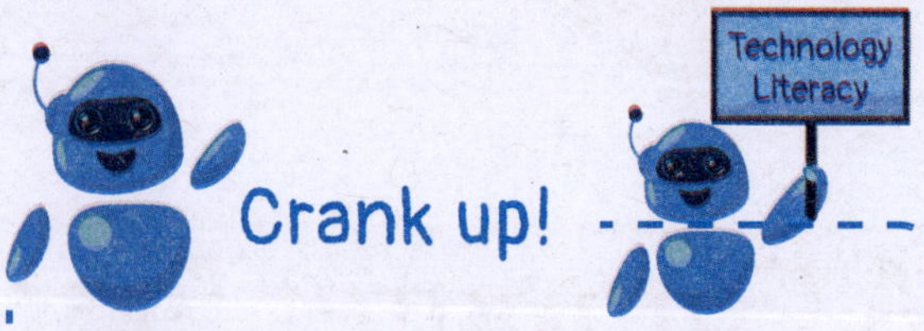

All computers are machines but not all machines are computers! Discuss in your class with the help of examples.

Computer System—Meaning

A computer has many parts. The various parts of a computer work together so that a computer can do various things. A computer will not be able to do anything without one or more of these parts. These parts together make up the computer system (Fig. 1.1).

A computer system has parts that can be touched and seen. These are called hardware. However, along with this, a computer also needs special programs, called software, to function. MS Paint is an example of a software program that helps us make drawings on a computer.

Fig. 1.1 | *A computer system*

An integrated system with a set of hardware and software devices is called a computer system. Let us learn more about hardware and software.

An integrated system with a set of hardware and software devices is called a computer system.

integrated: with various parts linked or coordinated

Hardware

Computer hardware refers to all the physical parts of the computer that we can touch. This includes all the parts, we can see and touch outside the computer, such as keyboard, mouse, monitor and the CPU. Hardware also includes the parts, we can see when we open the CPU box, such as the motherboard and CPU chips.

Keyboard, mouse, monitor, CPU and printer are some examples of hardware devices. We have already learned about them.

The parts of a computer that we can physically touch are known as computer hardware.

Let us discuss these in detail.

Soak up!

A hardware device that provides input to the computer is called an **input device**. Keyboard, mouse, scanner, microphone, joystick and webcam are some input devices that we have learned in the previous grades.

A hardware device that takes data from the computer and displays it to the user is called an **output device**. Speaker and Printer are examples of output devices.

Brush up!

Can you name the hardware parts of a computer and label them?

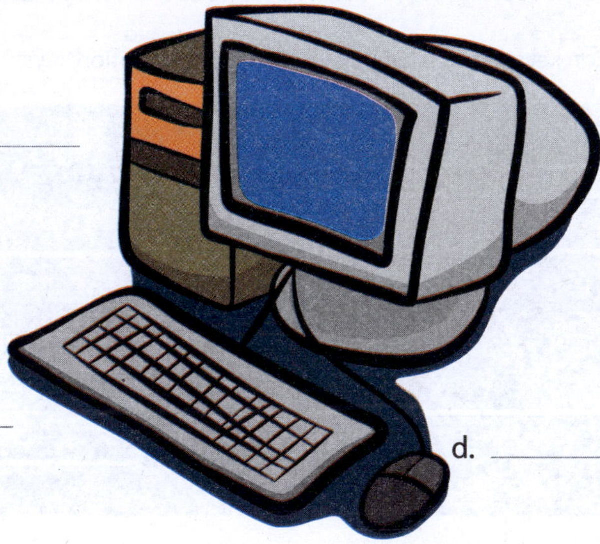

a. ____________________

b. ________________

c. ________________

d. ________________________

Monitor

The monitor looks like a TV because it has a screen. It displays the work done on the computer. We can read text and see movies and pictures on the screen. Monitors come in many different shapes and sizes.

There are two types of monitors:

1. Cathode Ray Tube (CRT) monitors
2. Thin Film Transistor (TFT) or flat-screen monitors

Fig. 1.2 | *Types of monitors*

Soak up!

A touchscreen helps us to give instructions to the computer by touching it. Mostly, tablets, mobile phones and ATMs have touchscreens. A stylus is a pen-like object that can be used with a touchscreen instead of fingers.

Keyboard

A keyboard is used to enter information into a computer. Without it, sending any information into the computer is difficult.

To write on a computer, we press the keys on the keyboard. This is called **typing**.

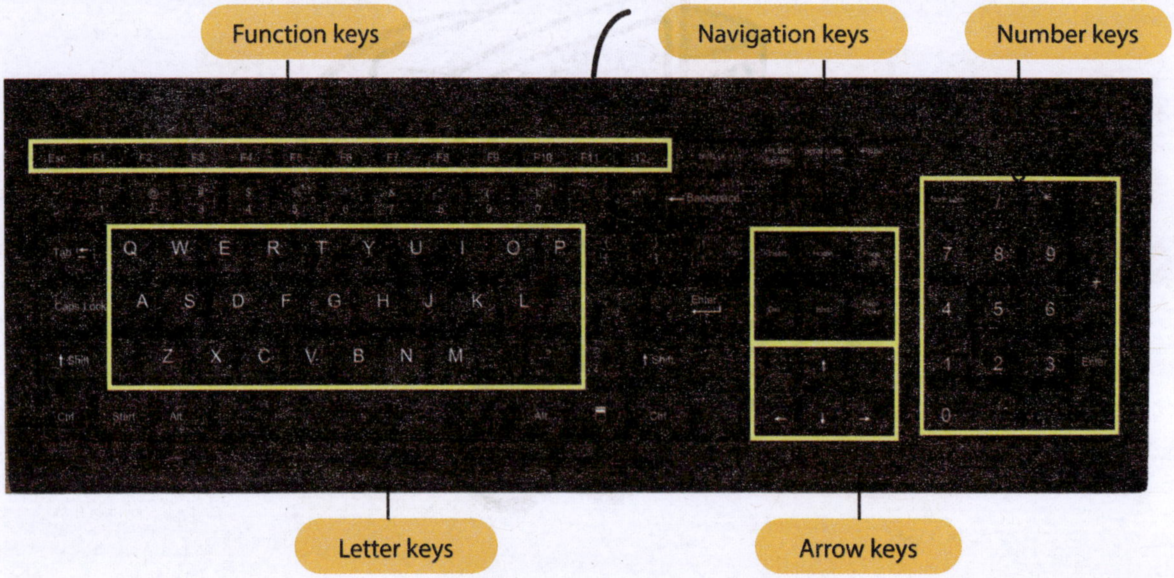

Fig. 1.3 | *Keyboard*

A keyboard includes alphabet keys, number keys, navigation keys, arrow keys, function keys and more keyboard keys, such as Shift, Caps Lock, Tab, Enter, Spacebar, Esc and Backspace.

Crank up!

Technology Literacy

The numeric keypad on the right is made to look like a calculator. The main typing keypad is how a typewriter used to be.

Soak up!

The first six letters in the first row of the letter keys are Q, W, E, R, T and Y. Thus, this keyboard is called the QWERTY keyboard.

Clear up!

The alphabet keys can be used to type both small and capital letters. Find out how.

Hint: Try using Caps Lock and Shift keys along with the letter keys.

Mouse

A mouse is a hardware device that is used to select, point, drag and drop objects on the screen. It has two buttons—*left* or primary button and *right* or secondary button, which help us select objects on the screen. There is a scroll wheel in between the two to move up and down faster. A mouse is usually kept on a mouse pad.

We can draw pictures, play movies and open files with the help of a mouse.

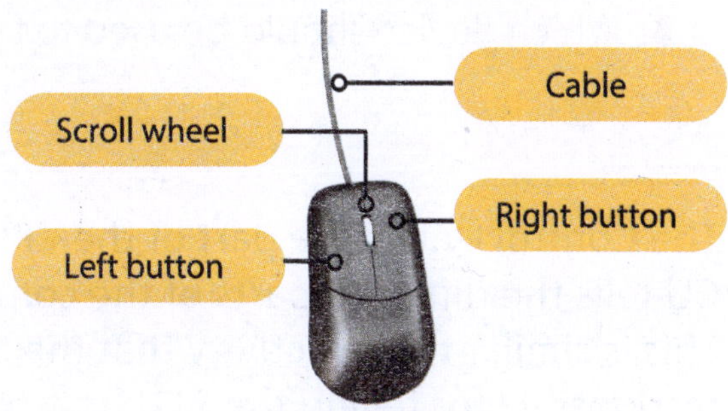

Fig. 1.4 | *Mouse*

CPU

CPU is the brain of the computer where the data processing happens. The full form of CPU is Central Processing Unit. Thus, it is called the **processor**. All the parts of the computer are connected to the CPU. It controls the other parts of a computer. It is also called the brain of the computer. The CPU box also consists of:

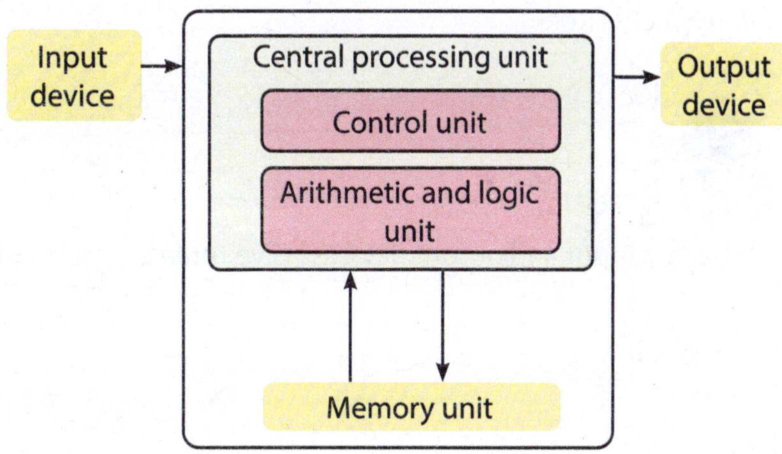

Fig. 1.5 | *Parts of a CPU*

1. the parts where the computer data is stored,
2. the button for switching the computer on and off, and
3. the place where we can attach external hardware devices.

The CPU is made of three main units, namely the Arithmetic and Logic Unit (ALU), the Control Unit (CU) and the Memory Unit (MU).

Brush up!

What the brain is to a human, the ____________ is to a computer.

Arithmetic and Logic Unit

The arithmetic and logic unit (ALU) does all the mathematical/arithmetic operations, such as addition and subtraction. It also performs logical operations. For example, it can arrange numbers in the ascending order and make decisions.

Examples of decision statements are:

- Is the sentence true or false?
- Which number is bigger?
- Which device should be used to take printouts?

Control Unit

The Control Unit is the part of the CPU that controls the input and output devices. The CU tells the different parts of the computer what to do. It assigns them their actions. This is similar to the activity that the brain does in the human body. The CU is mainly responsible for telling the ALU how to respond to the data or instructions received by the CPU.

The Memory Unit stores all the data that is to be processed. We will learn more about this in the next chapter.

Brush up!

What are input and output devices? Give three examples of each.

Printer

A printer prints information from the computer onto a sheet of paper. The sheet of paper with the information printed on it is called the **printout**. Printouts are also referred to as the hard copy of the information.

The most common types of printers are dot matrix printers, inkjet printers and laser printers.

Fig. 1.6 | *Printers*

Scanner

A scanner can read images or text from a physical item, such as a photograph or paper, and convert it into a form that the computer understands.

Fig 1.7 | *Scanner*

Speakers

Speakers help us listen to the sound played by a computer.

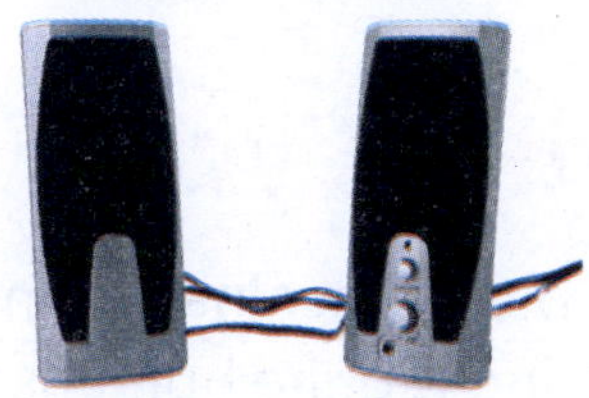

Fig 1.8 | *Speakers*

Software

In the human body, we can see and touch our hands and legs, but what really keeps us alive is breathing. Similarly, software keeps the computer alive. A computer is just an empty box without software programs in it. Software is a set of one or more programs that work together to help the computer perform a task. There are two types of software: system software and application software. Let us read more about them.

Software is a set of one or more programs that work together to help the computer perform a task.

System Software

It runs the computer hardware and the system. Windows operating system is an example of system software. It helps connect the computer hardware to the application software.

Application Software

These are programs that help users do certain tasks. For example, Tux Paint is an application software used to draw and save pictures on a computer.

Fun with AI

Artificial Intelligence is more of a software computer program rather than hardware. To run complex AI programs, computers use special hardware, such as graphics processor unit (GPU) and more advanced CPUs. These devices enable computers to run these programs more efficiently and quickly.

Brush up!

Discuss with your teacher and classmates about software. Write names of some application and system software.

System software: ________________________________

Application software: ________________________________

IPO Cycle

Most machines cannot run on their own and require humans to operate them. For example, a see-saw cannot move unless we push it, a washing machine cannot run unless someone switches it ON and a car cannot move until a driver drives it.

> Computers take the input from the users, process the input as per the instructions and give the output back to users. This order of steps is known as the IPO cycle.

Like all machines, computers cannot work on their own. We need to tell the computer what to do. After taking the input and instructions from the user, computers process the input data. After processing, they give the output to user. This order of steps is known as the Input-Process-Output (IPO) cycle. A computer always follows the IPO cycle. This is shown in Fig. 1.9.

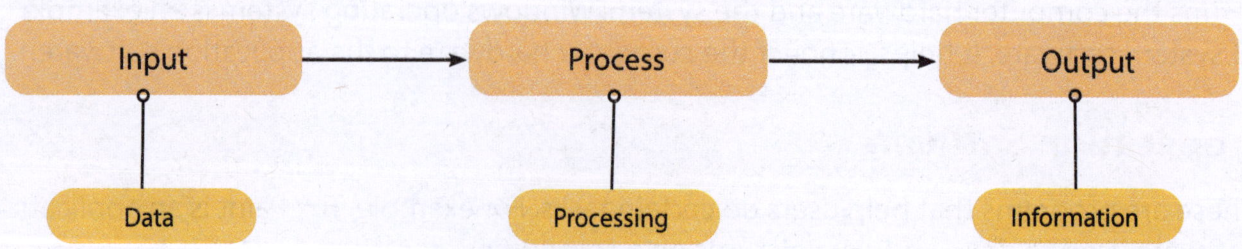

Fig. 1.9 | *The IPO cycle*

Working of the IPO Cycle

We know that a computer takes input from the user, stores and processes it, and shows the result.

> Data is the information processed by or stored in a computer. This information may be in the form of text documents, images, audio clips, software programs or other types of data.

The input can be taken in the form of data plus instructions. **Data** is information that is stored in and/or processed by a computer. **Instructions** tell the computer what to do with the data. Instructions can be mathematical or logical operations. Thus,

Input = *Data* + *Instructions*

For example, while using a calculator, we enter the operation 4 – 1. Here,

Input = *Data* (the numbers entered) + *Instruction* (the mathematical operation – (minus))

Output = Information (*the information it gives*)

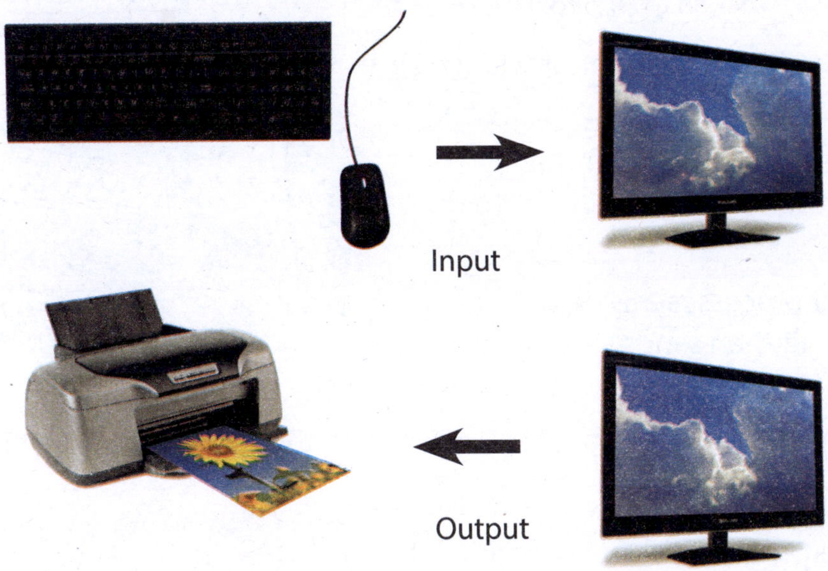

Fig. 1.10 | *Example of input and output*

Process

Sakshi wants to paint a picture of her pet dog on a canvas using watercolours. Here, the input is the watercolours, the output is the painting while drawing and colouring the picture of the dog is the process. Thus, the process is the action Sakshi takes from the start that results in the final output.

> Process is performing a certain task or action by the computer.

In a computer, the processing of data takes place in the **CPU**.

Hence, the user provides the input to the computer through an input device. Based on the input, the CPU performs various tasks and sends the result to the output device. The output device displays the result to the user.

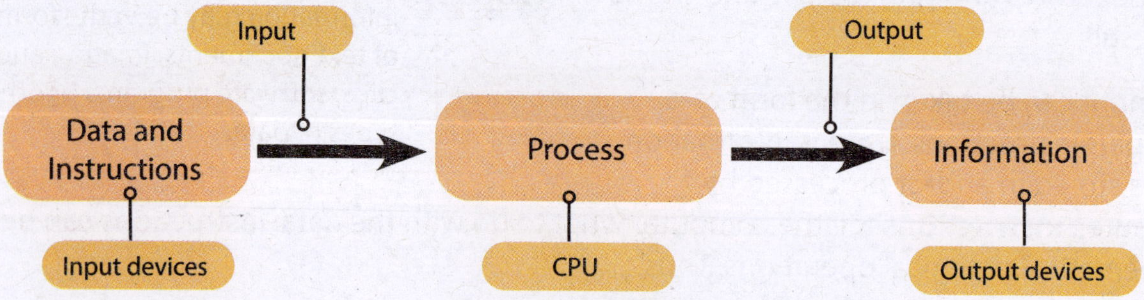

Fig. 1.11 | *Working of a computer using the IPO cycle*

Examples of the IPO Cycle

Let us look at more examples of the IPO cycle.

Displaying a Number on the Monitor

The steps to display '1' on the monitor (Fig. 1.12) are given below:

1. We type '1' on the keyboard (input device) and it sends a signal (input) to the computer.
2. The computer processes this data (in the CPU) and then sends a signal to the monitor (output device).

Fig. 1.12 | *Displaying a number on the monitor*

3. The monitor receives the signal and displays '1' to the screen or prints it using a printer (output).

Opening MS Paint

The steps to open MS Paint (Fig. 1.13) are given below:

1. Double-click on the Paint icon on the desktop (input) using a mouse (input device).
2. The computer processes this data (in the CPU).
3. The computer then opens the MS Paint application (output) on the monitor (output device).

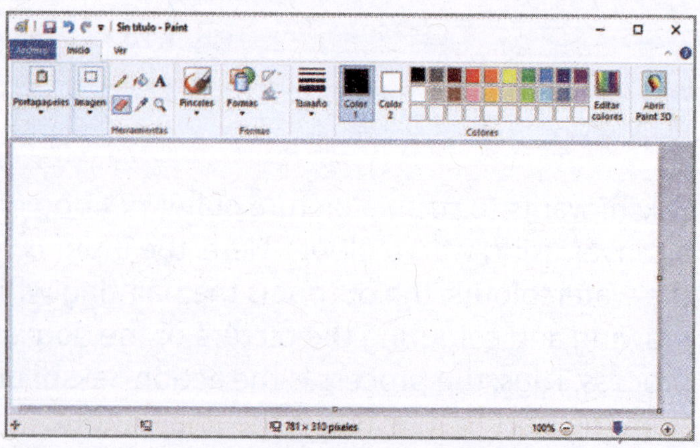

Fig. 1.13 | *Opening MS Paint*

Brush up!

Look at the following images. Write 'I' for an input activity, 'P' for a process and 'O' for an output activity.

1. 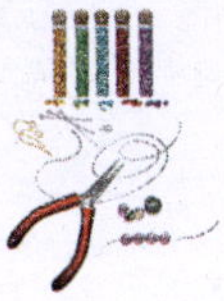  

2.   

Link up!

While playing games or using MS Paint, we give input to the computer by either moving the mouse or typing on the keyboard. After processing in the CPU, we get the output of the game or the drawing. All this is done in less than a second!

Today I learned!

- An integrated system with a set of hardware and software devices is called a computer system.
- The parts of a computer that we can see and touch are called hardware. Monitor, CPU, keyboard mouse, printer and speakers are all examples of hardware.
- Monitors can be of two types: cathode ray tube and thin film transistor.
- The CPU is made of two main units, namely ALU (Arithmetic and Logic Unit) and CU (Control Unit). The ALU does mathematical and logical operations. The CU controls the input and output devices and assigns them their Action.
- The parts of a computer that we cannot touch but are needed for the computer are called software. Software can be of different kinds.
- System software helps run the computer hardware and the system. Windows operating system is an example of system software.
- Application software are the programs that help users do certain tasks. MS Paint is an example of application software.
- Computers follow the input—process—output (IPO) cycle. The computer takes input, processes it and gives the output.
- Input is taken through input devices, while output is given through output devices. Processing happens in the CPU.

Revise and polish!

Learning Skills

1. Tick (✓) the correct answer.

a. Which of these is not a printer?

(i) Dot matrix ☐ (ii) Inkjet ☐
(iii) Laser ☐ (iv) Windows ☐

b. Which of these tasks is handled by the CPU?

(i) Data processing ☐
(ii) Controlling other parts of the computer ☐
(iii) Controlling the software ☐
(iv) All of these ☐

c. Which of these is another name for the CPU?

(i) Processor ☐ (ii) Brainy ☐
(iii) Communicator ☐ (iv) Central processing unique ☐

d. In which part of the computer are arithmetic operations carried out?

(i) Printer ☐ (ii) ALU ☐
(iii) Calculator ☐ (iv) CU ☐

e. _______________ means doing a certain action.

(i) Processing ☐ (ii) Acting ☐ (iii) Solving ☐ (iv) Printing ☐

f. Which of the following is used to take printouts of any work done on the computer?

(i) Printer ☐ (ii) Scanner ☐ (iii) CPU ☐ (iv) Monitor ☐

g. Which of the following devices is used to type text in the computer?

(i) Mouse ☐ (ii) Keyboard ☐ (iii) Scanner ☐ (iv) Printer ☐

h. Which of the following is an example of computer hardware?

(i) Webcam ☐ (ii) Paint ☐ (iii) Tree ☐ (iv) Windows ☐

i. Which of the following is an example of system software?

(i) Windows ☐ (ii) MS Paint ☐ (iii) Scanner ☐ (iv) Keyboard ☐

j. What is the full form of IPO?

(i) Input—output—process ☐ (ii) Input—output ☐
(iii) Input—process—output ☐ (iv) Process—input—output ☐

2. Fill in the blanks using the given words.

input scanner processor control unit output

a. The ____________ controls input and output devices and assigns them their action.

b. Data sent to the computer is known as ____________.

c. ____________ can read images or text from a physical document or image.

d. CPU is also known as the ____________.

e. ____________ is the processed information.

3. Rearrange the following in the correct order of the IPO cycle.

a.

☐

☐

☐

b.

☐

☐

☐

c.

☐

☐

☐

4. Rearrange the following words.

a. RPCUOTME ____________

b. INTRREP ____________

c. TDAA ____________

d. RESTOFAW ____________

e. ROTMINO ____________

f. POUUTT ____________

5. State whether the following statements are true (T) or false (F).

a. Scanner is a software program. ☐

b. A computer system includes only hardware devices. ☐

c. A computer can take input from the speaker. ☐

d. In a computer, the processing of data happens in the CPU. ☐

e. Devices that we can see and touch are called software devices. ☐

f. A mouse is an input hardware device. ☐

6. Draw the IPO cycle for the following.

a. Completing your homework

b. Making a sandwich

Lab Activity

Check the various hardware devices on the computer and see if you can touch all of them. Similarly, check the software programs on the computer and list down which ones are application software.

Think and Answer

1. Even our mobile phone is a computer. Can you think and tell which input device we use in our mobile phones?
2. Mrunal is learning to sing. She decides to record her first song and takes a mike and sings to record it on the computer. Which stage of the IPO cycle is she in? Draw the IPO cycle for this scenario.
3. Name the software applications used for the following.

   a. Software used to draw: ____________

   b. Software used to watch videos online: ____________

   c. Software used to type essays on a computer: ____________

   d. Software used to access the internet: ____________

Chapter

2

GUI Operating System—An Introduction

After reading this chapter, I will be able to:

- ✔ Describe the basic terminologies related to GUI.
- ✔ List different types of OS and their functions.
- ✔ Use various power modes of the computer.

Brainstorm and explore!

Information Literacy

Zoya and Jatin have gone for a picnic with their parents. Look at the given picture and answer the following questions.

1. How many family members do you see in the picture? ______________
2. Who is serving food to all family members? ______________
3. Who is cooking food? ______________

Our parents manage all the work at home. Similarly, a special software in all computers helps manage the working of all hardware and software resources. This software is known as the operating system.

The operating system is the link between hardware and software in a computer. After the computer is manufactured, it is loaded with an operating system. The operating system allows various applications to run on the computer. Windows and MacOS are two examples of the operating system.

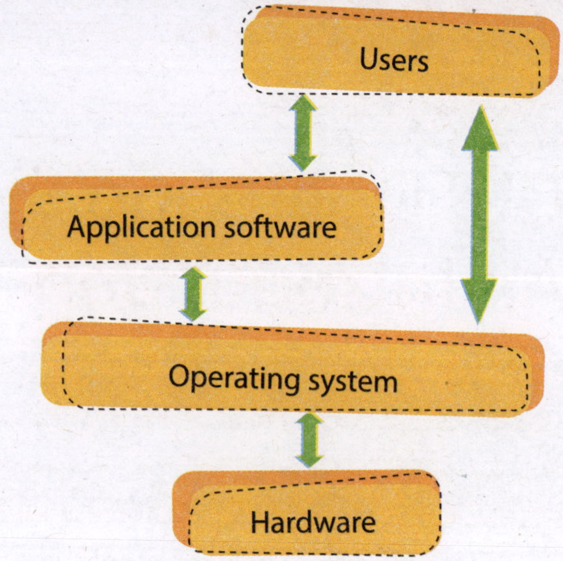

Fig. 2.1 | *Operating system*

Graphical User Interface

Once a computer with Windows operating system is switched ON, we can see elements, such as icons and text that allow the user to carry out a wide range of tasks easily. In the absence of a user-friendly screen organization, it would be difficult to use the computer.

As the name suggests, the user interface enables the user to interact with the computer. A graphical user interface uses visual elements, such as images and icons to enable the user to interact with the computer.

interface: common point between two things to ensure smooth working between them

A graphical user interface is an organized set of visual components that enables users to interact with the computer.

Windows and MacOS are some of the most widely used operating systems with graphical user interface. The other type of user interface is the command line interface. Here, the user has to enter commands to interact with the computer and see the output.

Crank up! (Technology Literacy)

The command line feature can be accessed on Windows devices with the help of the command prompt. To access it, type 'cmd' in the Search bar.

Soak up!

Apple II was the first computer with colour graphics and the QWERTY keyboard.

Introduction to Windows 10

Look at the following icons and tick the icon that appears first when you start your computer.

Microsoft Windows or Windows is the most popular operating system available for modern personal computers.

Microsoft created the Windows operating system in the 1980s. Over the years, there have been different versions of Windows, such as Windows 95, Windows 98 and Windows XP. The most recent versions are Windows 7, Windows 8.1 and Windows 10.

In this chapter, we will learn more about the basic features and working on Windows 10.

Windows Desktop and its Components

When we login to a computer with Windows 10, the first main screen that appears is the **desktop**.

The desktop has many components, such as icons, taskbar and so on.

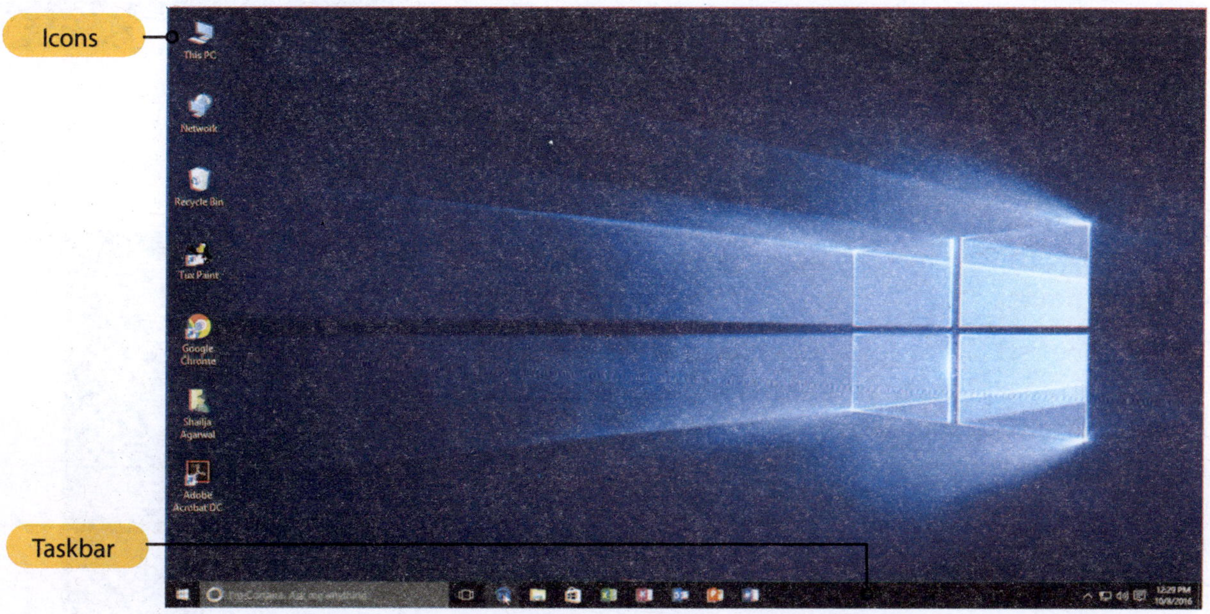

Fig. 2.2 | *Windows 10 desktop*

Icons

Fig. 2.3 | *Icon of Recycle bin*

The small pictures that we see on the desktop are called **icons**. Recycle Bin is one of the default desktop icons in Windows 10. It consists of all the programs and files that have been deleted or removed from the computer.

Taskbar

The Windows desktop consists of a bar at the bottom of the screen. This is called the **taskbar**. It consists of Start button, search bar, task view and notification area.

Fig. 2.4 | *Taskbar of Windows 10*

Start Button

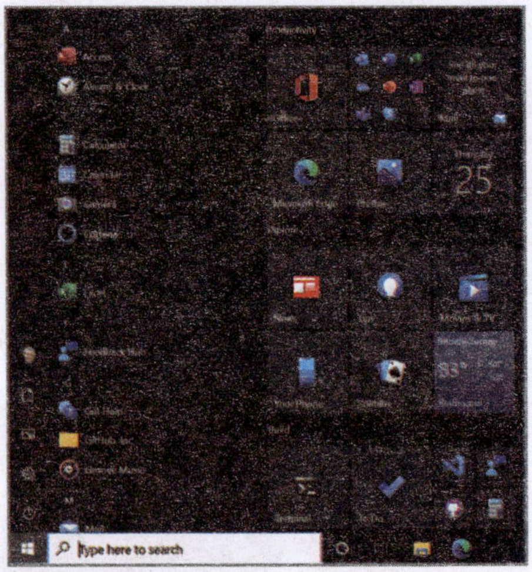

Fig. 2.5 | *Start menu*

The **Start menu** can be accessed using the **Start button**. It is present at the bottom-left corner of the taskbar. The Start menu gives access to all the applications or programs installed on the computer. These programs are arranged in the alphabetical order.

There are two ways to access the **Start menu**:

Left-clicking on the **Start** button with mouse.

Or

Pressing the **Windows** key () on the keyboard.

Soak up!

The Windows 10 Start menu has two panes: **Left pane** and **Right pane**.

The left pane lists all the applications installed on the computer in an alphabetical order. The right pane displays the applications on movable tiles. Some of the tiles can also be used to show information, such as date and temperature. Mostly, tiles are grouped on the basis of utility. The right pane was added for the users with touchscreen devices.

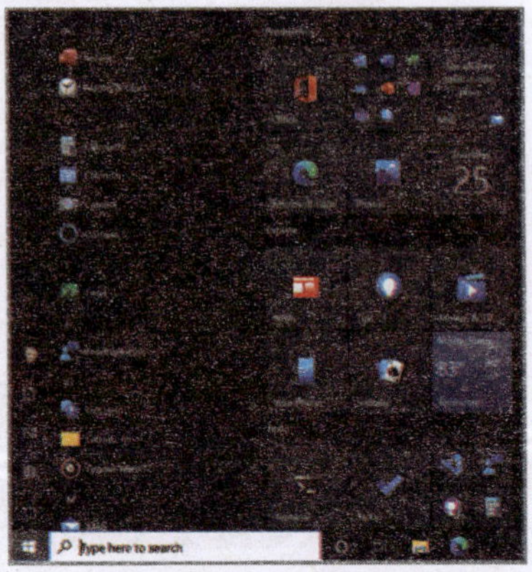

Search Bar

The search bar is also called the **Cortana bar**. It is a new feature of Windows 10. The search bar is used to search for a program, document, video or image on the computer.

Soak up!

Cortana is a virtual assistant created by Microsoft to help answer user questions. The operating system of Apple devices (iOS) uses Siri as their virtual assistant. Similarly, Alexa is Amazon's voice-based AI-powered digital assistant.

Clear up!

Go to the school computer lab and do the following tasks:

1. Calculate 14 + 35 using Cortana in the search bar.
2. Find the weather of your city using Cortana.

Task View

The task view helps us to see all the open windows quickly on the screen (Fig. 2.6).

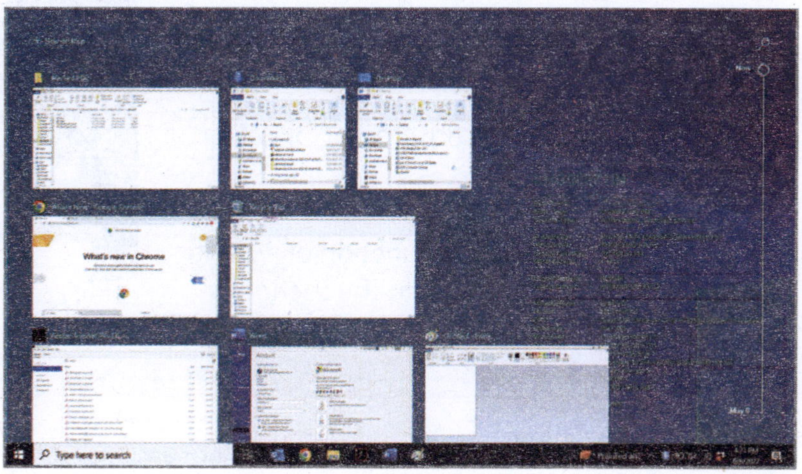

Fig. 2.6 | *Task view*

Notification Area

The notification area is located at the right side of the taskbar (Fig. 2.7). It is also called the status area. It shows the status of functions, such as the internet connection, time, battery status, volume level, etc.

Fig. 2.7 | *Notification area*

A few icons are visible on the Notification area. We can see more icons by clicking on the upward sign beside the notification area.

The taskbar also shows all the active applications on the desktop. Every active application is indicated by a green underline. It also shows the pinned applications. For example, upon clicking the  icon on the taskbar, Microsoft Edge (the web browser application in Windows 10) is opened.

Soak up!

The small vertical line on the rightmost end of the taskbar helps us minimize all the open windows and show the desktop.

Pin/Add an Application to the Taskbar

We can add frequently used programs and files to the taskbar for easy access. This is called **pinning** a file or an application to the taskbar (Fig. 2.8). Pinning applications also helps to keep the desktop clean. We can also unpin the applications when not in use.

These are the steps to pin an application to the taskbar:

1. In the Start menu, search for the application you want to pin.
2. Right-click on the application.
3. Click on the **More** option at the top of the menu.
4. Click on the **Pin to taskbar** option.

This will add or pin the required application icon to taskbar.

pinning of application: the function of adding a shortcut to the applications to the section

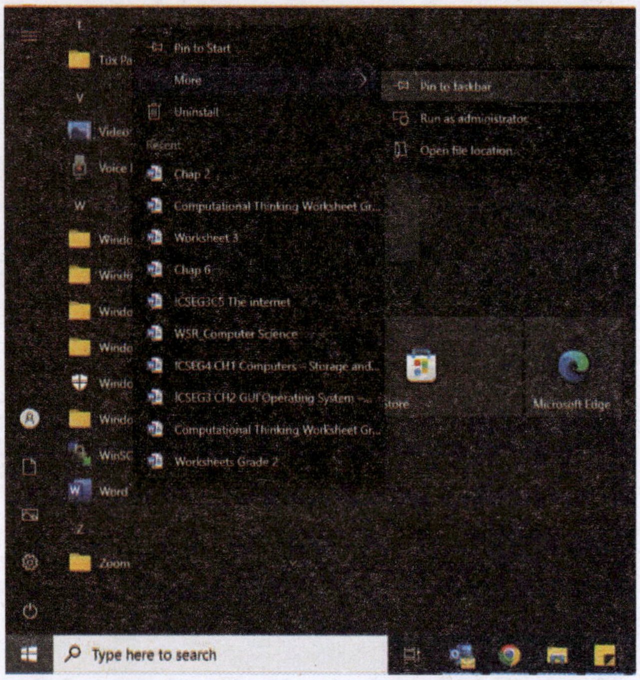

Fig. 2.8 | *Pin/Add application to the taskbar*

Soak up!

'Pinning' is a very useful feature of Windows 10 that enables users to access frequently used applications with a single-click, without cluttering the desktop.

Crank up!

Technology Literacy

Windows 10 has a lot of keyboard shortcuts that can save time in performing actions. Let us learn about them.

Task	Shortcut key
Opening a new browser window	Ctrl+N
Switching between windows	Alt+Tab
Locking the computer	Windows key+L
Closing a window	Alt+F4
Opening the task view	Windows key+Tab

Basic Operations on the Desktop

The desktop is the first screen that we see after turning on a computer. The desktop has various functions that help us change the look and feel of it. Let us learn about some of them.

Adding a Shortcut to the Desktop

By adding icons to the desktop, important and frequently used applications can be accessed easily. This is called **creating the shortcut to the application**.

The steps to add a shortcut to the desktop are as follows:

1. Right-click anywhere on the desktop.
2. Click on the **New** option and then click on the **Shortcut** option.
3. Browse for the application or file you want to create a shortcut to and click on the **Next** button.
4. Assign a name to the shortcut and click on the **Finish** button.

A new icon will be visible on the desktop window. Similarly, the shortcut for folders and files can be created on the desktop.

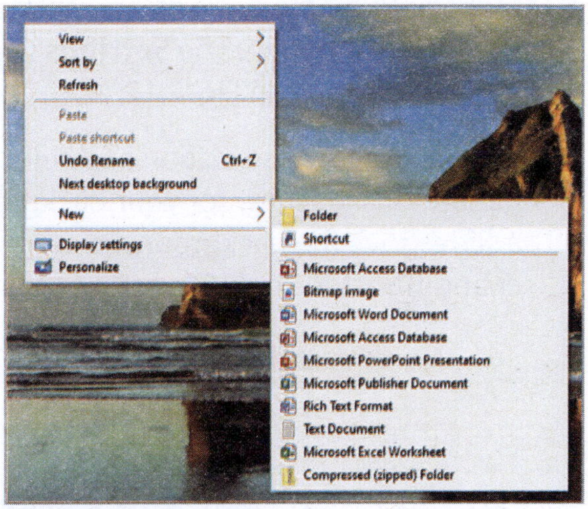

Fig. 2.9 | *Adding a shortcut to the desktop*

Opening a Program using Icons

To open a program, double-click on its icon.

Moving and Arranging Desktop Icons

Desktop icons can also be dragged around on the screen. They can be made smaller/bigger by right-clicking on the desktop, going to the **View** option and then selecting the size of the icons.

The icons can be sorted alphabetically according to their name, size, type or latest date modified. To do so, right-click on the desktop, click on the **Sort by** option and then click on the required option. Users can also arrange the icons manually on the desktop according to their preference.

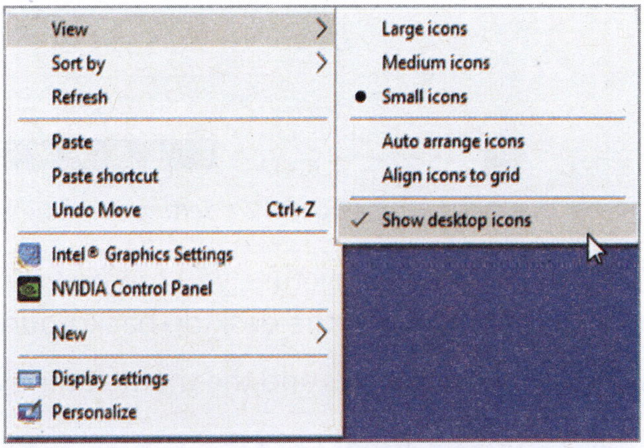

Fig. 2.10 | *Rearranging and resizing the desktop icons*

Changing Desktop Background

We have seen the default Windows 10 background. It is same as the Windows 10 icon. We can change the background image as per our wish.

default: a particular set of instructions which a computer always uses unless the person using the computer gives other instructions

The steps to change the Windows background are given here:

1. Right-click on the desktop and click on the **Personalize** option. The **Settings** window will appear as shown in Fig. 2.12.
2. Click on the Browse option and select a picture or slideshow for your background. In a slideshow, the background picture keeps changing after a definite period of time.

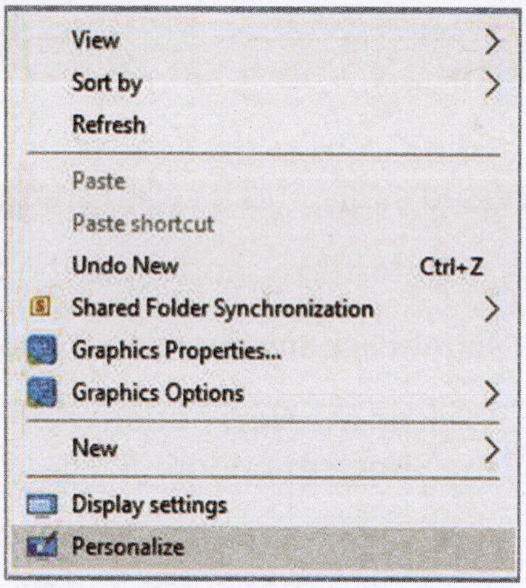

Fig. 2.11 | *Clicking on the Personalize option*

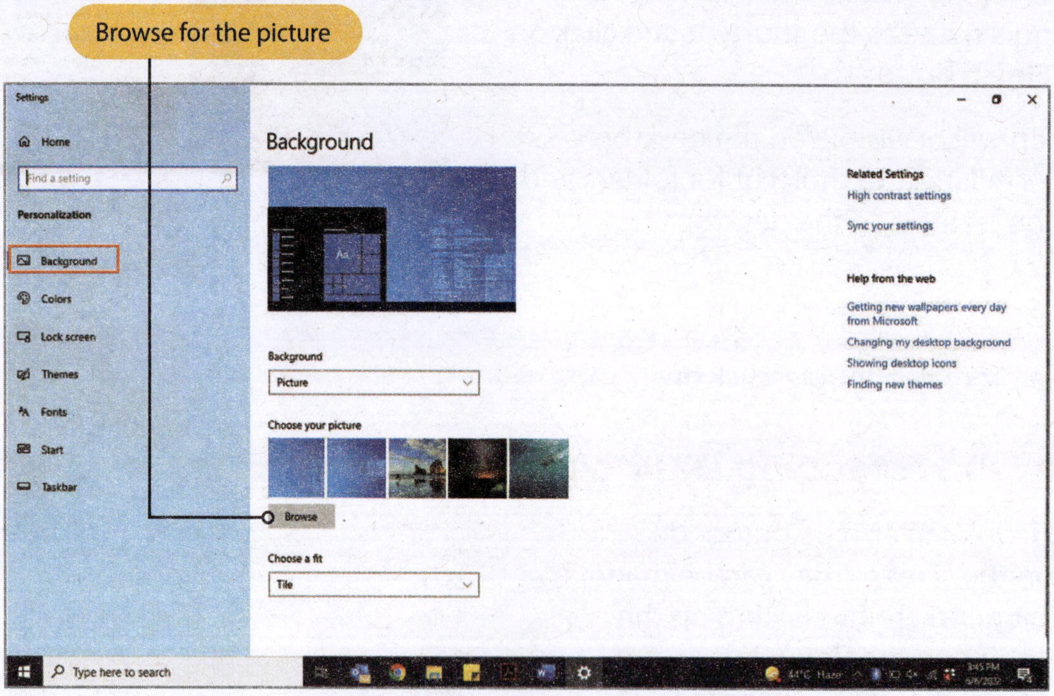

Fig. 2.12 | *Settings window with Personalized option selected*

3. After choosing a picture, you can preview the selected background. The selected picture will set as the desktop background or the wallpaper.

Similarly, colours, fonts and the theme of the background can also be changed.

wallpaper or background of the desktop: a decorative image that appears on the back of the screen behind the icons

Changing the Screen Saver

As shown in Fig. 2.11, there is one more option called **Display settings** above the **Personalize** option. This option is used to change the brightness of the computer and adjust the volume of the speaker and microphone. It has additional options as well to check other features of the computer. Explore them in the computer lab.

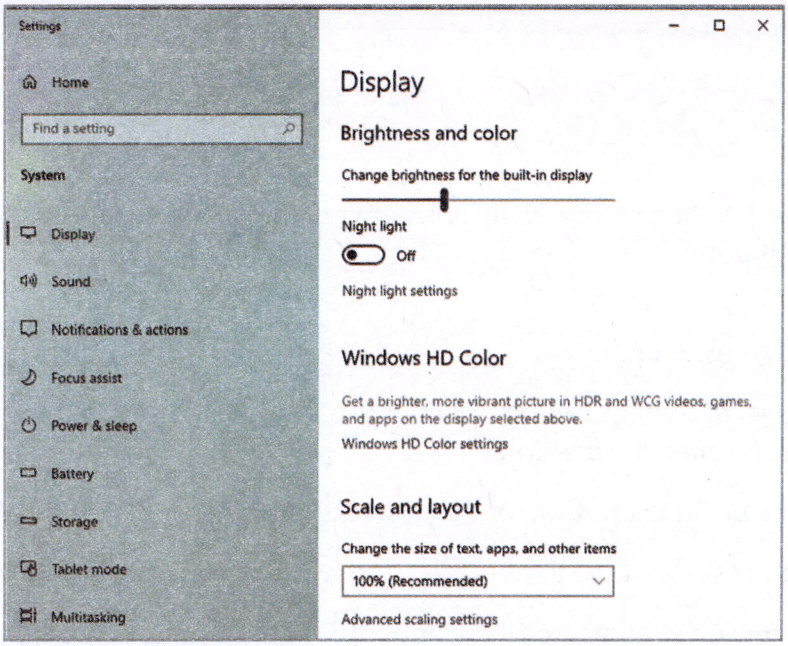

Fig. 2.13 | *Settings window with the Display settings option selected*

Modes in Windows 10

The default mode of Windows 10 is the **Normal mode**. It is the usual functionality of Windows.

When the PC is not shut down properly or has some related issues, Windows opens in the **Safe mode**. Safe mode enables users to operate Windows in a safe state, that is, with a limited set of functionalities. If there are issues, they can be troubleshooted in the safe mode.

To change the power mode quickly, select the **Battery** icon on the taskbar and then drag the slider to the power mode you want.

In order to avoid any errors or system failures, it is of utmost importance to shut down the computer and turn it on properly. Ensure all applications are closed before shutting the computer down.

Soak up!

The **Lock screen** option on the **Personalize** window lets us choose the display picture when the computer is in the locked state.

Clear up!

Just like changing the desktop background, can you change the colour of the taskbar using the Colors option in the Personalize window?

Today I learned!

- The operating system is the link between the hardware and the software of a computer.
- A graphical user interface is an organized set of visual components that allows users to interact with the computer.
- When we login to a computer with Windows 10 operating system, the first main screen that appears is called the desktop.
- Taskbar is the bar at the bottom of the desktop window.
- The taskbar consists of the Start button, Search bar, Task view and Notification area.
- The Start menu gives access to all the applications or programs installed on the computer. It consists of two panes: left pane and right pane.
- Search bar is used to perform a variety of tasks, such as searching for a program, application, document on the computer, playing music, etc.
- Task view allows the user to see all the open windows quickly on a single screen.
- Notification area shows the status of functions, such as the internet connection, time, battery status or the volume level.
- We can change the background image by right-clicking on the desktop and selecting the Personalize option.
- The Display settings option can change the brightness of the computer and adjust the volume of the speaker and microphone.
- To add a shortcut to a file or an application on the desktop, right-click on the desktop. Click on the New option and then click on the Shortcut option.
- Windows opens either in the Normal mode or in the Safe mode.

Revise and polish!

1. Tick (✓) the correct answer.

a. What is the first main screen of the Windows 10 called?

(i) Icon ☐ (ii) Taskbar ☐ (iii) Desktop ☐ (iv) Menu ☐

b. Which of the following notifies about the internet connection?

(i) Task view ☐ (ii) Start menu ☐

(iii) Notification area ☐ (iv) Right pane ☐

c. Which of the following is used to change the desktop background?

(i) Personalize window ☐ (ii) Display settings ☐

(iii) Wallpaper ☐ (iv) Home ☐

d. Which of the following options is used to increase the size of the desktop icons?

(i) View ☐ (ii) New ☐

(iii) Display settings ☐ (iv) Size up ☐

e. Which of the following options is not contained in the taskbar?

(i) Open applications ☐ (ii) Pinned applications ☐

(iii) Settings ☐ (iv) Notification area ☐

2. Fill in the blanks using the given words.

Display settings search Tab Start menu Taskbar

a. The ______________ bar is used to quickly search for programs.

b. When we click on the Start button, the ______________ appears.

c. The ______________ shows all active applications on the desktop.

d. The keyboard shortcut to open the task view is Windows + ______________ key.

e. The ______________ option is used to change the brightness of the computer.

3. Match the following.

a.	Default mode	(i)	Safe state
b.	Start button	(ii)	Search bar
c.	Safe mode	(iii)	Normal
d.	Cortona bar	(iv)	Adjust the volume of the speakers
e.	Display settings	(v)	Windows key

4. State whether the following statements are true (T) or false (F).

a. Windows, is the most popular operating system. ☐

b. The small pictures that we see on the desktop are called buttons. ☐

c. The Start menu can be accessed using the Start button. ☐

d. The search bar is also called the Cortana bar. ☐

e. The notification area is located at the left side of the taskbar. ☐

5. Write the actions for the following keyboard shortcuts.

a. Windows key+Tab ____________________

b. Alt+Tab ____________________

c. Ctrl+N ____________________

d. Windows key+L ____________________

e. Alt+F4 ____________________

Experiential Learning

Lab Activities

Go to the computer lab and switch ON the computer. Now, perform the following tasks:

1. Change the background picture of the desktop.
2. Open the MS Paint application from the Start menu and create its shortcut on the desktop.
3. Move the taskbar to the top of the desktop, as shown here:

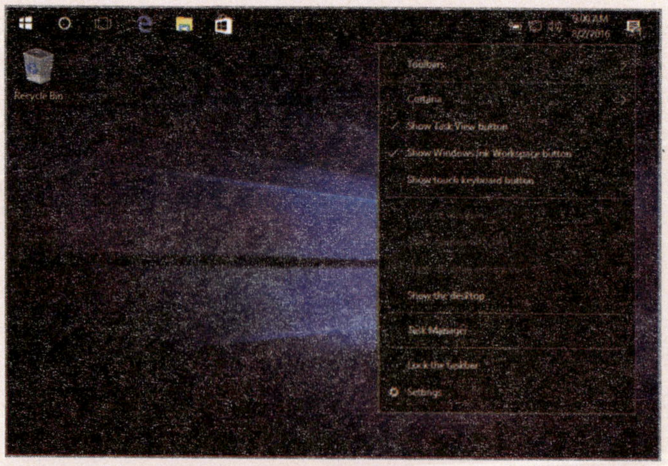

Hint: Search for the **Lock the taskbar** button.

Chapter 3

Word Processor—An Introduction

After reading this chapter, I will be able to:

- ✔ Identify different parts of the MS Word window.
- ✔ Open, close and print a document.
- ✔ Create and save a document.

Brainstorm and explore!

The city of Wonderland has an old ice-cream factory. When it was started, the owners wrote the ingredients and the recipes in small notebooks. In a few years, they had more than a hundred notebooks with details of ingredients for different flavours, cone designs and so on. It was getting out of hand. So, the owners decided to buy a computer to store these records. Which software, do you think, would best suit their purpose?

Using a software program will help the owners to save the recipes and records as documents without the fear of them getting stained or lost.

When we want to create a text document, such as a recipe, a story or a letter on a computer, we use a word-processing program.

A word-processing software application is used to create, edit and print text documents. WordPad, WordPerfect and Microsoft Word (MS Word) are some examples of word-processing software. In this chapter, we will learn the working of MS Word 2016 in detail. MS Word is usually pre-installed in a Windows laptop or PC. For other devices, such as iPad and MacBook, MS Word can be downloaded from the AppStore.

Microsoft Word is a software application from the Microsoft Office suite used to create, edit and print text documents.

Starting MS Word 2016

There are two ways to start the MS Word application on a computer.

To open MS Word from the Start menu, click the **Start** button and then select **Word** (Fig. 3.1).

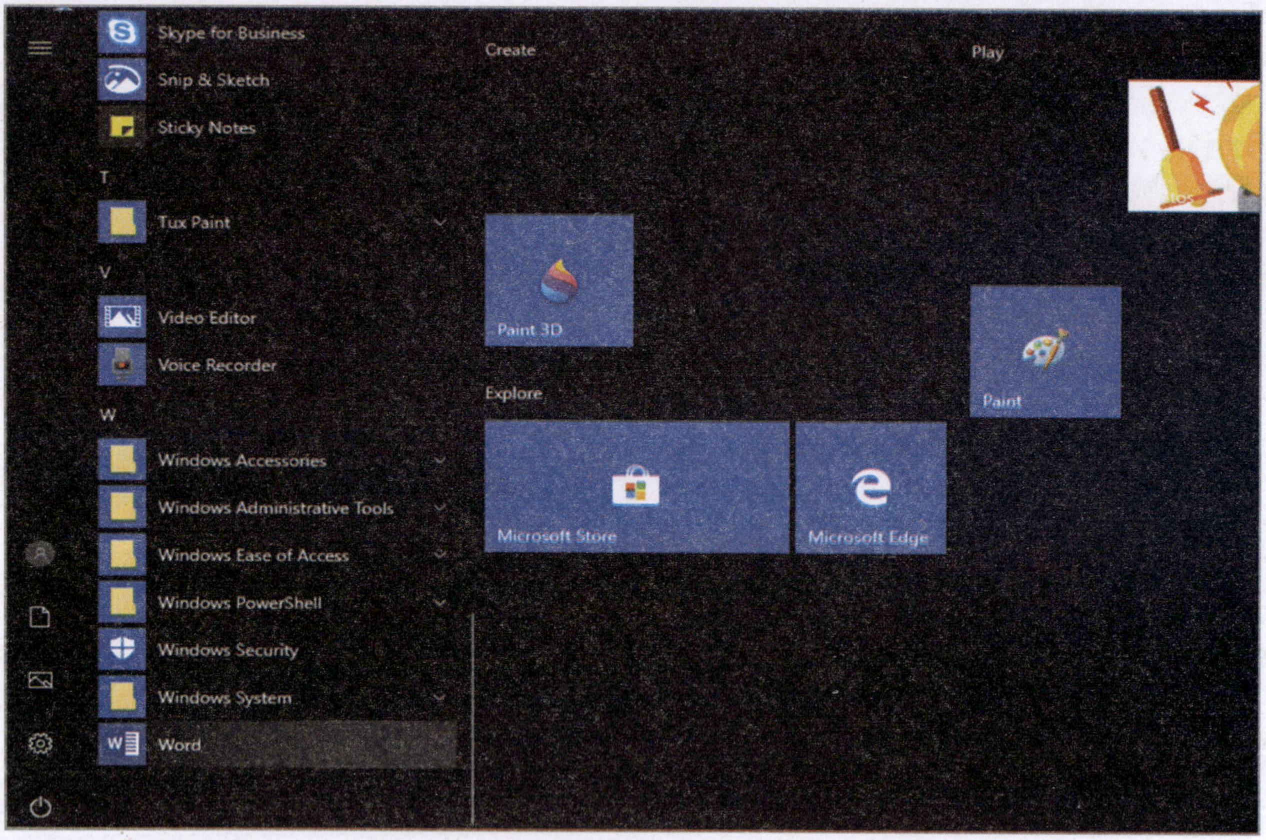

Fig. 3.1 | *Opening MS Word using the Start button*

OR

Press the Windows key ( ) + **R** on the keyboard. In the dialog box, type '**winword**' → press **Enter** (Fig. 3.2).

The MS Word window will appear, as shown in Fig. 3.3. Select **Blank document** option and start creating documents.

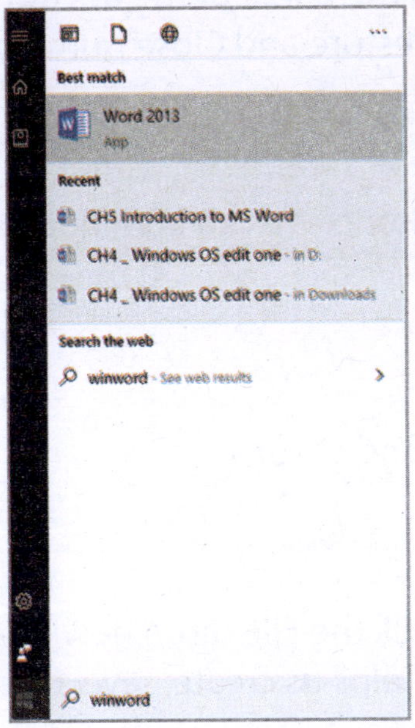

Fig. 3.2 | *Opening MS Word by typing 'winword'*

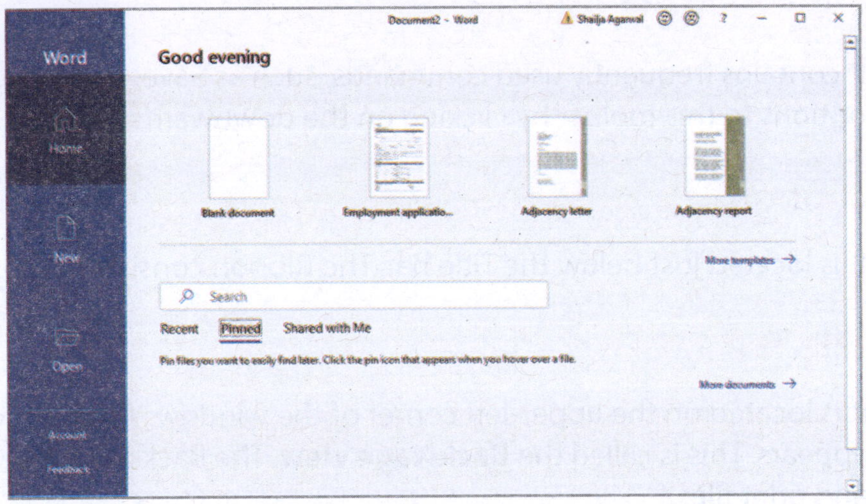

Fig. 3.3 | *MS Word 2016 window*

Parts of MS Word 2016 Window

The main parts of MS Word window are shown in Fig. 3.4.

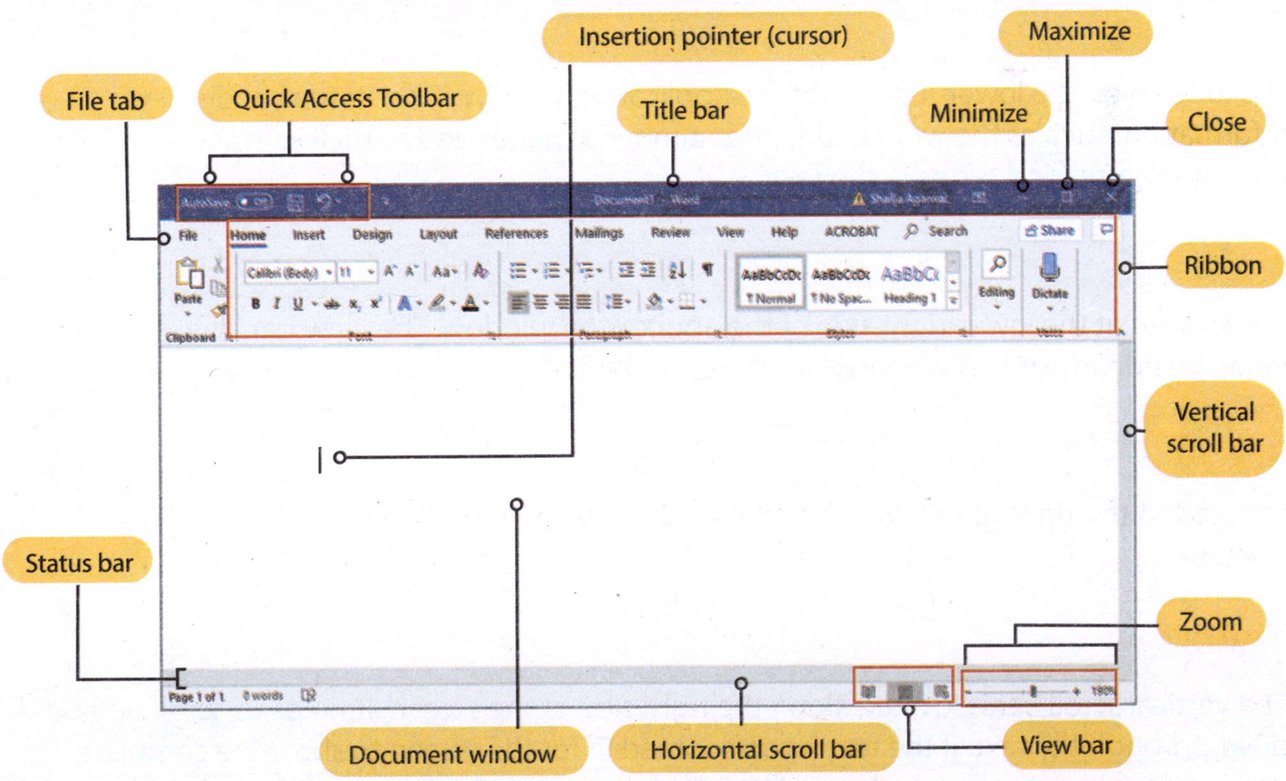

Fig. 3.4 | *Main parts of MS Word window*

Title Bar

It is a horizontal bar located at the top of the window. It displays the name of the document. The right side of the title bar contains the Minimize, Maximize/Restore and Close buttons.

Quick Access Toolbar

It contains frequently used commands, such as Save, Undo and Redo. We can add more options to this toolbar by clicking on the downwards arrow.

Ribbon

It is located just below the Title bar. The Ribbon consists of tabs and groups.

File Tab

It is located on the upper-left corner of the window. When we click the File tab, a new screen appears. This is called the **Backstage view**. The Backstage view helps us create, save, open and print files.

Document Window

This is the area where the text is typed or edited. The vertical blinking line indicates where the typed text will appear in the document window and is known as the **cursor**.

Status Bar

It is located on the lower-left side of the application window. The status bar displays information, such as the word count, the number of pages and a small icon showing if there are any grammatical errors in the text.

View Bar

It is located at the lower-right side of the application window. The view bar allows users to view the document in different modes, such as Web Layout, Print Layout and Read mode.

Zoom Tools

Located to the right of the view bar, the zoom tools help us set the zoom level of the document.

Scroll Bar

The vertical scroll bar is located along the right side of the screen. It helps us scroll up and down through the text. If the text is too zoomed in for the screen to show the complete document, a horizontal scroll bar appears just above the status bar, which can be used to navigate left or right.

Creating a New Document

After starting MS Word, the application starts with a new document. To open another new document while the application window is open, follow the steps given below:

1. Click on the **File** tab.
2. Select the **New** option.
3. Click on **Blank document.**

A new document will open.

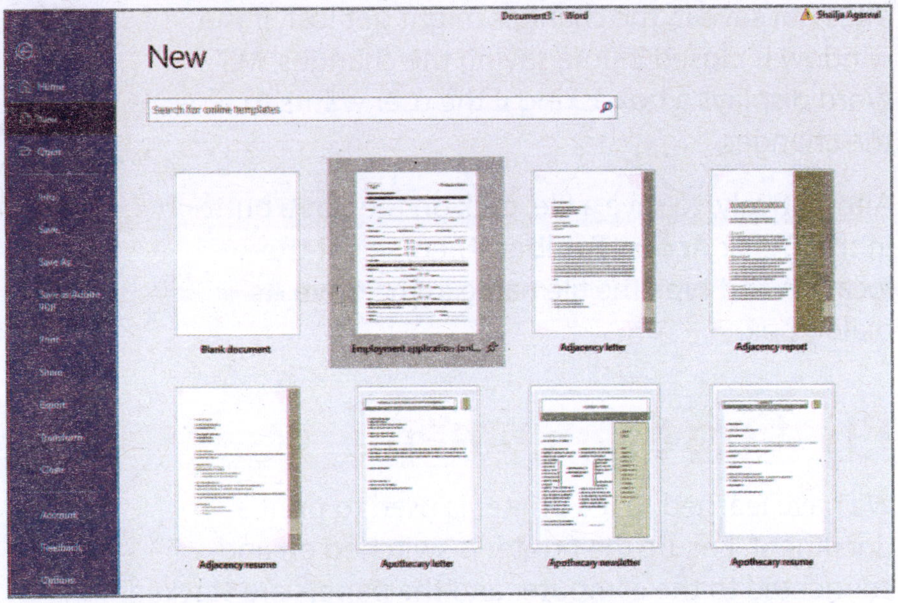

Fig. 3.5 | *Select blank document from the available templates*

Saving a Document in MS Word

To save a document in MS Word, follow the steps given below:

1. Click on the **File** tab.
2. Select the **Save As** option (Fig. 3.6). From the Save As dialog box, select the desired folder.
3. Type the name of the file in the **File name** text box.
4. Click on the **Save** button.

The **Save As** option is used to save the file with a file name in a desired folder on the computer. The **Save** option is used to save the changes made while editing a document.

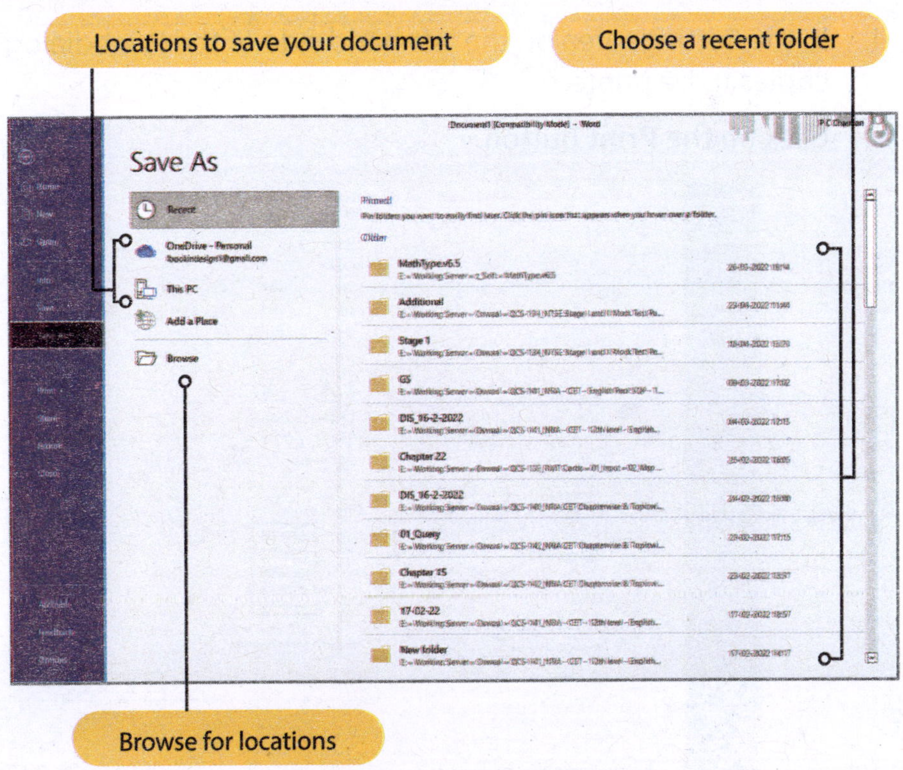

Fig. 3.6 | *Saving a document*

For example, if one has already saved a file in a location and then adds a few paragraphs but does not save it, the changes might get lost. If the window is closed before saving the changes, MS Word displays a box asking if the user wants to save the changes.

Alternatively, to save a file, click on the **Save** button in the **Quick Access Toolbar**. Then, select the location and type the file name in the **Save As** dialog box.

Technology Literacy

Crank up!

To open a new document, the keyboard shortcut is Ctrl+N. To save a document, it is Ctrl+S.

Printing a Document

We have learned that a printer is used to print a document. Ensure the printer is switched on and connected to the computer and the papers are stacked. After this, follow the steps given below:

Soak up!

We must only print when absolutely necessary, in order to save paper.

1. Click on the **File** tab.
2. Select the **Print** option.
3. In the preview on the right-hand side of the Print dialog box, check the Page Setup Properties.
4. In the Settings area on the left-hand side of the Print dialog box, select the number of copies to be printed.
5. Click on the **Print** button.

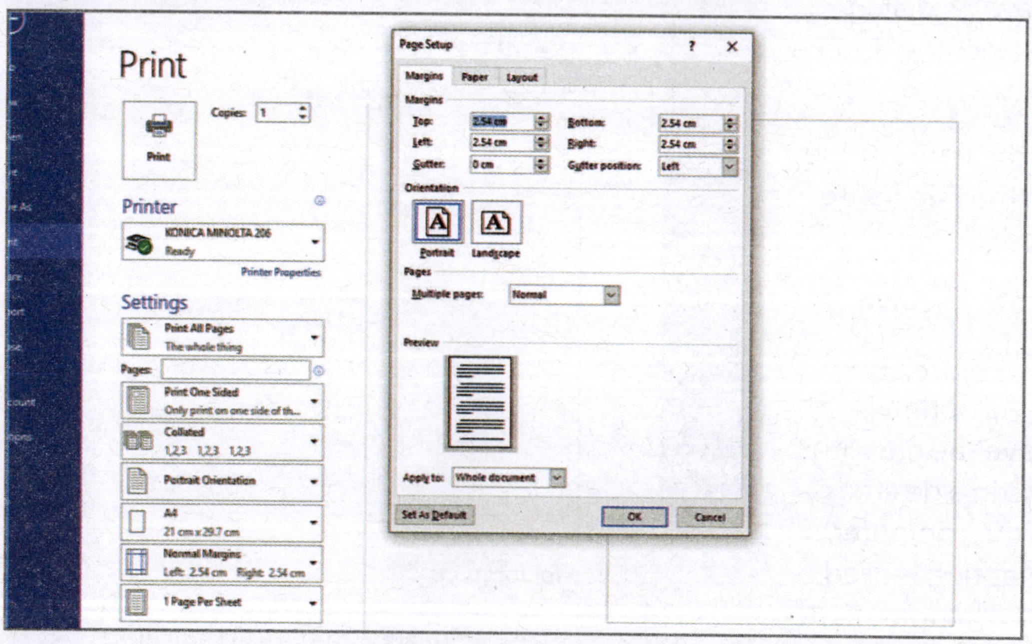

Fig. 3.7 | *Printing a document*

Opening an Existing Document

If MS Word is already open, we can open an existing file saved on the computer by following these steps:

1. Click on the **File** tab.
2. Select **Open** option and browse the folder in which the file you want to open is located.
3. Click on the file you want to open. Once the file is selected, the name of the file will be displayed in the File name text box.
4. In the Open dialog box, click the **Open** button. The document will be displayed in the document window.

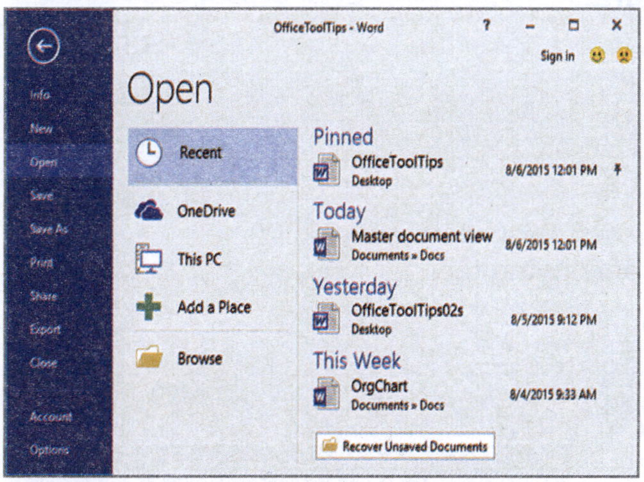

Fig. 3.8 | *Opening an existing document*

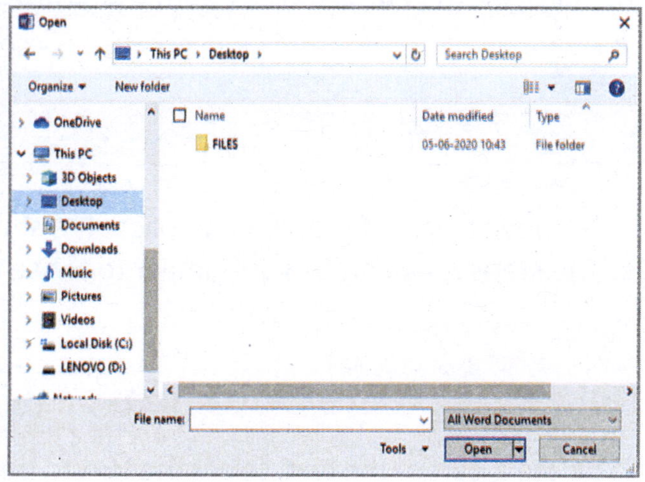

Fig. 3.9 | *The Open dialog box*

To open the document if the MS Word window is not open, double-click on the file in the folder which contains it.

Text in an MS Word Document

Once the document is open, we can start typing the text in the document area. MS Word provides various options to do so.

Selecting Text in a Document

We can select text using the keyboard or the mouse. The blank area to the left of the typed text is known as the selection area. To select text, click where you want to begin the selection from, then hold the left mouse button, and drag the pointer to the point you want to select (Fig. 3.10).

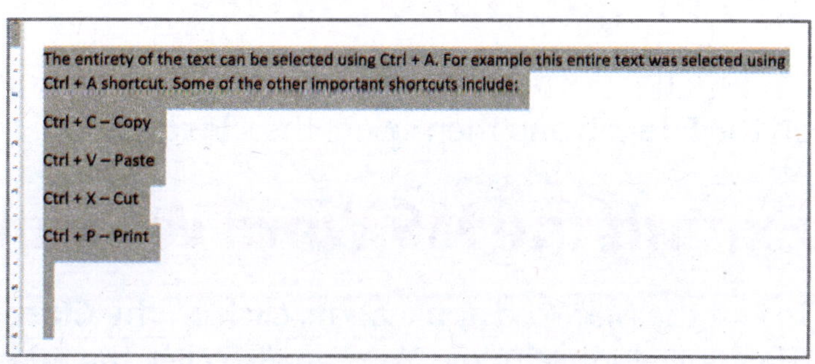

Fig. 3.10 | *Selecting text*

Copying Text in MS Word

Copying text means creating a duplicate of the original text and leaving the original as it is. To copy text and paste it elsewhere, follow the steps given below:

1. Select the text to be copied.
2. Click the **Copy** button in the **Clipboard** group from the **Home** tab.
3. Place the cursor at the location where you want to paste the copied text (it can even be placed in another Word document).
4. Click on the **Paste** button from the **Clipboard**.

Fig. 3.11 | *Using the Copy option from the Clipboard*

Crank up!

To move a part of the text and paste it elsewhere, we use the Cut option. The steps for using this are similar to those for copying text.

Deleting Text in a Document

To delete a part of the text, select the text to be deleted and then press the **Delete** or **Backspace** key on the keyboard.

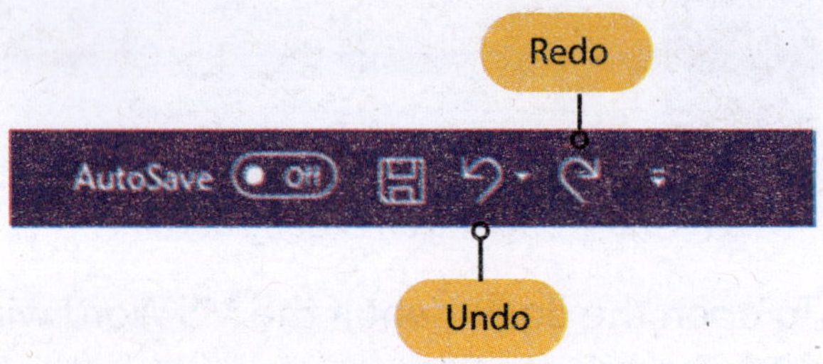

Fig. 3.12 | *Undo and Redo buttons*

Using Undo and Redo Options

The **Undo** and **Redo** buttons are available on the **Quick Access Toolbar**.

- The **Undo** button is used to cancel the last action performed.
- The **Redo** button is used to reverse the actions of the **Undo** button.

Closing a Document

To close the document window in MS Word without closing the application window, click on the **File** tab and then select the **Close** option.

Exiting the MS Word Window

To exit the MS Word application, click on the **Close** button located at the top-right corner of the application window. You can also click the **File** tab and then select the **Exit** option.

If the document that is being closed is not saved, an MS Word warning message appears asking whether you really want to close the file without saving it.

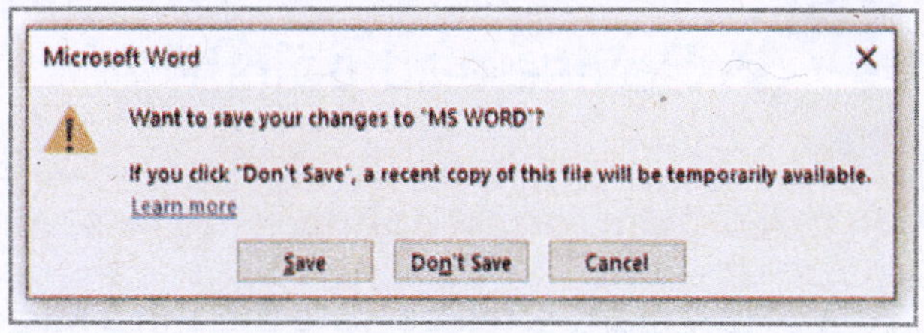

Fig. 3.13 | *Warning message to save a document*

Technology Literacy

Crank up!

Some important keyboard shortcuts in MS Word 2016 are given below:

Action	Keyboard Shortcut
To reach the beginning of the line	Home key
To reach the end of the line	End key
Open a document	Ctrl+O
Print a document	Ctrl+P
Cut	Ctrl+X
Copy	Ctrl+C
Paste	Ctrl+V
Undo	Ctrl+Z
Redo	Ctrl+Y

Today I learned!

- MS Word is a word-processing software. It is used to create, edit and print text documents.
- The main parts of MS Word window are Title bar, Quick Access Toolbar, Ribbon, File tab, Status bar, View bar, Zoom tools, and Horizontal and Vertical scroll bars.
- To open a new document or an existing file and to save or print a document, click on the File tab and select the respective option.
- To select text, use the keyboard or the mouse.
- We can Cut, Copy, Paste and delete text in an MS Word document using the shortcuts or the drop-down menu.
- It is important to save changes before closing the window or exiting an MS Word document.

Revise and polish!

1. Tick (✓) the correct option.

a. How many scroll bars are there in a Microsoft Word 2016 document?

(i) One ☐ (ii) Two ☐ (iii) Three ☐ (iv) Four ☐

b. ____________ is the shortcut to save a document.

(i) Ctrl+S ☐ (ii) Ctrl+D ☐ (iii) Ctrl+P ☐ (iv) Ctrl+E ☐

c. How many view buttons are present in a Microsoft Word 2016 document?

(i) Three ☐ (ii) Four ☐ (iii) Five ☐ (iv) Six ☐

d. ____________ is the small vertical blinking line that appears on the screen when typing a text.

(i) Pointer ☐ (ii) Cursor ☐ (iii) Click ☐ (iv) Tab ☐

e. The menu of ____________ tab is also called the Backstage view.

(i) File ☐ (ii) Home ☐ (iii) Insert ☐ (iv) View ☐

f. Which of the following buttons is used to cancel the last action performed?

(i) Save ☐ (ii) Undo ☐ (iii) Redo ☐ (iv) Print ☐

g. The process of creating a duplicate of the original text and leaving the original text as it is called ____________.

(i) cutting ☐ (ii) pasting ☐ (iii) copying ☐ (iv) printing ☐

h. What is the blank area to the left of the typed text called?

(i) Selection area ☐ (ii) Blank area ☐

(iii) Text area ☐ (iv) Selected area ☐

i. Which of these views helps us create, save, open and print files?

(i) Design view ☐ (ii) Layout view ☐

(iii) Backstage view ☐ (iv) Edit view ☐

j. Which of the following are examples of word-processing software?

(i) WordPad ☐ (ii) WordPerfect ☐

(iii) MS Word ☐ (iv) All of the above ☐

2. Give the uses of the following in MS Word 2016.

a. File tab

b. Document window

c. Status bar

d. Scroll bars

3. **Fill in the blanks using the given words.**

copy   Exit   document   print   Quick Access

a. MS Word is a word-processing software and is used to create, save and __________ text documents.

b. Text is typed or edited in the __________ window.

c. To exit MS Word, click on the __________ button.

d. We can cut, __________ and paste text in MS Word.

e. The Undo, Save and Redo buttons are on the __________ Toolbar.

4. **Match the following.**

a.	New file	(i)	Ctrl+X
b.	Open file	(ii)	Ctrl+N
c.	Cut	(iii)	Ctrl+V
d.	Copy	(iv)	Ctrl+C
e.	Paste	(v)	Ctrl+O

5. **Answer the following questions in brief.**

a. What is MS Word?

b. How do you open an MS Word document saved on the desktop?

c. What are the steps to copy a paragraph and paste it?

d. What are the steps to print a document?

e. What are the different kinds of information that can be written using the MS Word?

Lab Activities

1. In the lab, locate all parts of the MS Word application window.
2. Type the following details about yourself in MS Word:
   a. Name   b. Birthday   c. School name
3. Make documents for the following in MS Word:
   a. Days of the week   b. Months in a year   c. Numbers from 1 to 20
4. Write a letter to your best friend telling him/her about your holidays.

Chapter

4

An Introduction to the Internet

After reading this chapter, I will be able to:

- ✔ Describe the internet and its uses.
- ✔ Describe the advantages and disadvantages of the internet.
- ✔ Describe important terms related to the internet.
- ✔ Describe how to stay safe while using the internet.

Brainstorm and explore!

Cross Curricular

Fill in the blanks with the words given below.

crowd school bouquet internet

1. 

Group of flowers

____

2. 

Collection of fish

____

3. 

Group of people

____

4. 

Network of computers

____

When many computers are connected together, it is called a network. A global network of computers connected to each other is called the internet.

What is the Internet?

All of us use the internet every day, but do we really know what the internet is?

The internet is a worldwide network of computers.

The internet, also called the net, connects millions of computers across the world. A computer user can exchange any information with another computer user via the internet. It provides all kinds of information and communication services.

History of the Internet

The internet was first invented for military purposes. Then, it was made available to scientists. Gradually, it was made available to everyone.

It was co-invented on January 1, 1983 by Vinton Cerf and Robert Kahn, who are also known as **fathers of the internet**. It was a result of an experiment called the ARPANET by the US Department of Defense in the late 1960s. Later, ARPANET turned into what is now called the modern internet in 1983.

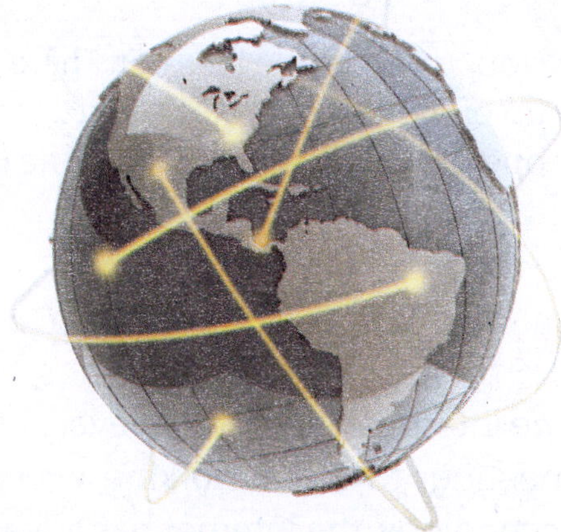

Fig. 4.1 | *The internet*

Uses of the Internet

The internet enables us to do many things. Some of them are:

- Browsing websites and applications for information
- Sending and receiving messages/emails for personal and professional use
- Accessing online classes or courses
- Downloading apps, software and their updates
- Playing games online
- Shopping online via e-commerce
- Connecting socially with other users through social media websites and applications
- Storing information, such as photos, videos and documents on the web repository

Soak up!

Electronic commerce or e-commerce is the activity of buying, selling and exchanging goods and services over the internet. Each business process, such as performing transactions, exchanging data and terms of sale, is performed electronically.

Brush up!

Explain in your own words what the internet is.

____

____

Soak up!

Nobody owns the internet. There is no central agency that manages it. The internet is made up of multiple networks, which are managed by multiple independent local operators. Each operator handles its share of the local system.

Advantages and Disadvantages of the Internet

The internet has changed every aspect of our lives. From online classes, banking, shopping, meetings to online working, everything has been made possible by the internet. Like any other technology, the internet has advantages and disadvantages, too. Let us learn more about them.

Advantages of the Internet

The internet is one of the best inventions till date and, it has made our lives easier in so many ways. Here are some advantages of using the internet:

1. The internet contains vast amounts of information. When properly used, we can get information on any topic from the internet.
2. The internet has made it easy for people to connect with others. People living across the world can communicate with each other via audio or video calls, or simply chat in a matter of seconds using the internet.
3. The internet can also be used to watch movies or listen to songs, read the latest news, etc.
4. Shopping for books, clothes, shoes, medicines, bus, train or airplane tickets is possible through the internet.
5. The internet has made it possible to share pictures, videos and other information with other people in a matter of a few seconds through email or social media without the use of any specialized devices.

Brush up!

Can you name any app used for sending pictures online?

____

Disadvantages of the Internet

The internet needs to be used carefully and within limits. Here are some disadvantages of using the internet:

1. Once we connect to the internet, we should be careful about the sites we click on. Some websites can infect our computers with a virus. They try to attack our computers and steal our personal information. This is why, we should never download any files from an unknown source.
2. We can get a lot of unwanted emails from strangers or advertisements from companies, which may contain viruses or can simply slow down the system.
3. The internet is a vast source of information. Browsing the internet within limits is enjoyable. But, many people get addicted to the internet, which wastes a lot of their time.
4. The internet has a lot of false information that usually spreads fast, causing problems. We should trust news from reliable sources only.
5. Sometimes, we share personal information, such as address, phone numbers and pictures on the internet, which can be misused by strangers.
6. It is very easy to connect with other people on the internet. However, we must be careful not to share any personal information or pictures with other people over the internet. This information can be misused by other. This is called cyberbullying.

> A virus is a software program that is downloaded into the computer without one's knowledge and can cause harm to it in multiple ways.

> Cyberbullying is to threaten or trouble someone on social media platforms or over email by sending them unpleasant messages.

Important Terms Related to the Internet

Here are some important terms related to the internet that we should know:

Webpage

A webpage is a single document that can be opened on the web browser. This page contains text, images, videos and links to other webpages. A webpage is part of the website.

> A link on a webpage that connects to another page is called a hyperlink.

Website

A website is a page or collection of webpages on the internet that contains specific information. If a website is a complete book, a web page is just a page in that book. To search for any information, we usually open a website.

For example, www.google.com or www.harpercollins.com or www.mindchamp.in are called the web addresses that are used to open the respective websites.

Fig. 4.2 | *A webpage on a website*

Home Page

The first page of the website is called home page. This page usually contains important information about the website and has links to other pages on the website.

Soak up!

Websites are written in a special language called HTML. The person who writes this is called a programmer.

Search Engines

Just like a dictionary helps us find out the meaning of new words, a search engine is a program that helps users search for information on a specific topic on the internet. Examples of search engines include Google, Yahoo and Bing. It can be used to find any information about a specific topic on the internet, collect information for school projects, etc. We can search for information using keywords or images.

keywords: a set of one or more words used to look up more information on a specific topic

Crank up! Technology Literacy

Google is the most popular website used in the world. Flipkart is a popular Indian online shopping website.

Brush up!

If you have a school project to find information on the Indian freedom fighters, where will you go to look for information? Give the steps for the same.

____

____

____

____

Opening a Webpage

We use the address of a person to locate the person in a city. Similarly, websites also have an address that is used to locate them on the internet. This address given to a web page/ website is called the uniform resource locator (URL) or the website address. To open a webpage, follow these steps:

1. Open a web browser, such as Google, Firefox or Safari.
2. Place the cursor on the address bar on top of the web browser.
3. Enter the website address you wish to open. Let us consider, www.harpercollins.com
4. Press Enter.
5. The Harper Collins home page will open.

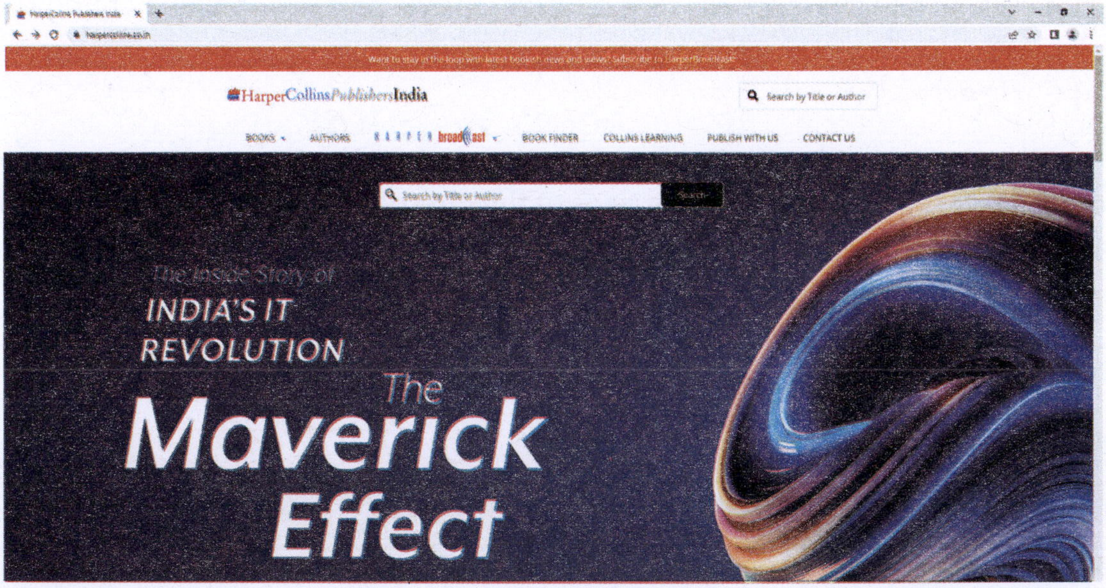

Fig. 4.3 | *Website opened*

Fun with AI

Search engines use artificial intelligence to identify the search results that will be most useful to the user. This means that if you, your teacher and your parents search using the same keywords, the search results will not be identical for all of you. Try it out for yourself!

Soak up!

Once you start typing in the address bar, it usually suggests the website address. In case an incorrect address is entered, the default search engine results will open.

Online Safety

We can take the following steps to be safe online:

1. Do not set an easy password. Try to use different passwords for different websites.
2. Do not share your password with anyone.
3. Shop only from secured sites. Check that the URL has the https protocol.
4. Do not click on pop-ups.
5. Be careful while using public Wi-Fi.
6. Do not click on any random links sent by strangers via emails or online gaming sites.

Digital Citizen

Today, internet and technology affect many aspects of our life. We are as much citizens of the internet as we are of our country. Citizens of the internet are also called **digital citizens** or **netizens**.

A person who uses the internet regularly is called a netizen or a digital citizen.

Just as good citizens abide by laws and ethics, good netizens also follow ideal practices. To be a good netizen, one must:

1. Be respectful to everyone online,
2. Never create fake identity or steal someone's identity,

3. Report to parents/teachers while seeing anything wrong or illegal on the internet, and
4. Never copy anything without the owner's permission.

Fig. 4.4 | *A netizen*

Today I learned!

- The internet is a worldwide network of computers.
- The internet is used by billions of users to access websites, send emails, communicate with each other, use social media, educate themselves, shop, play games, and download software and updates.

  Internet has a lot of advantages and disadvantages at the same time.
- World wide web or www is a collection of web pages.
- A webpage is a single document that can be opened on the web browser.
- A website is a page or collection of webpages on the internet that contains specific information.
- The first page of the website is called the home page.
- A search engine is a program that helps users search for more information about any topic on the internet. Users can search using keywords or pictures.
- A web browser is a software used by a user to access the www. Examples are Internet Explorer, Chrome, Safari and Firefox.

Revise and polish!

Learning Skills

1. Tick (✓) the correct answer.

a. What is the global network of computers called?

(i) Internet ☐ (ii) Network ☐

(iii) Virus ☐ (iv) Computer system ☐

b. Which of the following is used to search for information about a specific topic on the internet?

(i) Search engine ☐ (ii) Home page ☐

(iii) Website ☐ (iv) Web page ☐

c. Users can access the internet using the __________ application.

(i) web browser ☐ (ii) home page ☐

(iii) search engine ☐ (iv) Paint ☐

d. To access a particular website, one needs to type the __________ in the address bar.

(i) webpage ☐ (ii) home page ☐ (iii) URL ☐ (iv) home ☐

e. Who is known as the father of the internet?

(i) Charles Babbage ☐ (ii) Cerf and Kahn ☐

(iii) Bill Gates ☐ (iv) Grace Murray Hopper ☐

f. What is the first page of a website called?

(i) Web page ☐ (ii) Home page ☐ (iii) First page ☐ (iv) URL ☐

g. Which one of these is not a search engine?

(i) Google ☐ (ii) Bing ☐ (iii) YouTube ☐ (iv) Yahoo! ☐

h. Which of the following cannot be done using the internet?

(i) Booking airplane tickets ☐ (ii) Buying new shoes ☐

(iii) Paying school fees ☐ (iv) Shaking hands ☐

i. What is the full form of URL?

(i) Uniform resource location ☐ (ii) Unified resources location ☐

(iii) Uniform representation of location ☐ (iv) Uniform resource locator ☐

j. A __________ is a collection of webpages.

(i) home page ☐ (ii) website ☐

(iii) search engine ☐ (iv) hyperlink ☐

2. **Fill in the blanks using the given words.**

social media   URL   internet   spam   passwords   hyperlink

a. Emails and ____________ applications are some of the ways through which we can connect to others over the internet.

b. Vinton Cerf and Robert Kahn are also known as the fathers of the ____________.

c. https://www.irctc.com is an example of a ____________.

d. We should never share our ____________ with others.

e. We can get a lot of unwanted emails from strangers in the form of ____________.

f. A ____________ enables users to move from one web page to another.

3. **State whether the following statements are true (T) or false (F).**

a. The internet was first created for the military. ☐

b. It is okay to share personal details with everyone on the internet. ☐

c. We can share our password with our best friend. ☐

d. Chrome is an example of web browser. ☐

e. We need the internet to send emails to friends. ☐

4. **Rearrange the following words.**

a. NTINERET ____________

b. BWRSORE ____________

c. BCUYLBLEYRING ____________

d. PGEAHMEO ____________

e. CHOMRE ____________

5. **Answer the following questions.**

a. What are the advantages of the internet?

b. What is the internet? Give two uses of the internet.

c. Give three ways to stay safe online.

d. Describe three disadvantages of using the internet.

e. Give the differences between a website and a webpage.

Lab Activities

Experiential Learning

1. You can set your default search engine on the web browser. Ask your teacher how to do it.
2. Go to the computer lab and type the websites given below and see if these are opening:

   youtube.com   www.mhrd.gov.in   https://amazon.in
3. Get more information about the Indian winners in Olympics. Can you search the internet for this?

Group Activity

Collaboration

1. In groups of four, research by talking to family and friends to find the ways to stay safe on the internet. Create a Word document for the same.

Think and Answer

Critical Thinking   Problem-solving

1. Girish has recently created a new email id. He received an email from an unknown person saying he has won a lottery of 100000$. Should he open it?
2. Ajit is getting abusive messages from one person in his gaming chatroom. What should he do?
3. Divya just got a new computer. Can you guide her by numbering the steps to access the Amazon website?
   a. Open Microsoft Edge.
   b. Type www.amazon.com in the address bar.
   c. Download antivirus software.
   d. Press Enter.
4. Help Tanuja by underlining in green the steps to take in order to stay safe on the internet and underline in red the things she should avoid.
   a. Download an antivirus application.
   b. Create a fake identity.
   c. Share password with mom.
   d. Click on random pop ups while browsing the internet.
   e. Set password to 12345.
   f. Download the attachment sent via email by her dad.
   g. Open an email sent by a friend inviting to his/her birthday.
   h. Shop from website whose URL begins with http.

Chapter

5

Fun with MS Paint

After reading this chapter, I will be able to:

- ✔ Explain how to select images.
- ✔ Define how to use the Clipboard group.
- ✔ Discuss the tools present in the Image group.
- ✔ Explain the uses of the Tools group.

Technology Literacy

Brainstorm and explore!

In the previous grade, we have learned how to use MS Paint to draw and colour on the computer. MS Paint files are saved as images. But, what happens after we save the images? What can we do with them?

Look at the following pictures. Fill in the blanks using the given words.

email **print** **show**

a. We can __________ pictures to our teachers

b. We can __________ pictures to our friends.

c. We can __________ pictures to make a photo album.

Selecting an Image

Sometimes, we need to move a part of the drawing or move the text from one part to another. The **Select** tool is used to select the entire drawing or a part of it.

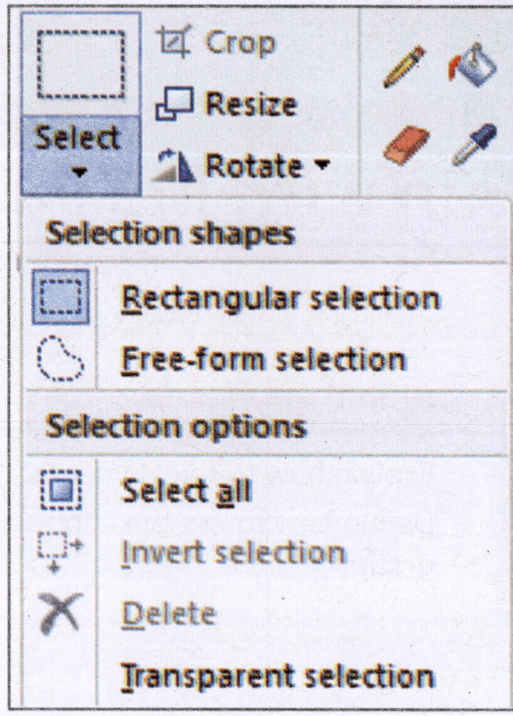

Fig. 5.1 | *Select tool drop-down menu*

To select the entire drawing, follow the steps given below:

1. Click on the **Select** tool drop-down arrow from the **Image** group of the **Home** tab.
2. The drop-down menu shows two selection shapes, namely **Rectangular selection** and **Free-form selection**. Based on the shape selected, the **Select** tool gives us various options to choose from.

   Rectangular selection: This option is used to select a rectangular or square area of the image.

   Free-form selection: This option is used to select an object of any shape by dragging the mouse around the shape.

Fig. 5.2 | *Selecting part of an image*

Clear up!

Under the **Select** tool, there are four more options. These are: Select all, Invert selection, Delete and Transparent selection. Explore these and find what they do.

Clipboard Group

The Clipboard group is present under the Home tab of the MS Paint application. It consists of three tools: Cut, Copy and Paste (Fig. 5.3).

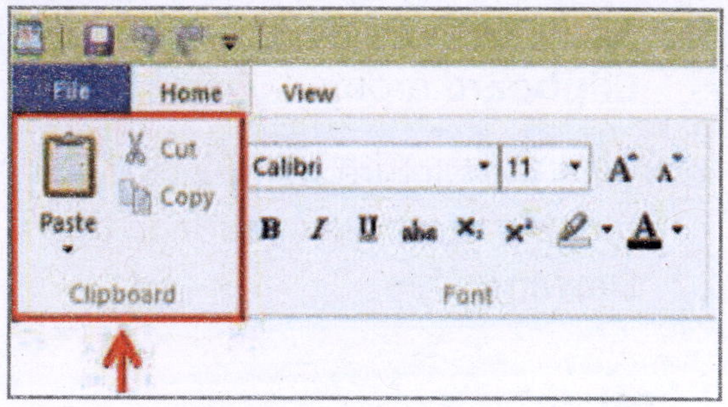

Fig. 5.3 | *Clipboard group*

Cutting and Pasting an Image

The **Cut** option takes out the selection that can then be pasted. To cut a picture or a part of it and paste it in another part of the picture, follow the steps given below:

1. Select the part of the drawing you want to cut by using the **Select** tool in the **Image** group.
2. Click on the **Cut** option in the **Clipboard** group.
3. Click on the **Paste** option in the **Clipboard** group.
4. With the picture still selected, move it to a new location in the Drawing Area.

Fig. 5.4 | *Cutting and pasting an image*

Copying and Pasting an Image

The copy option makes a copy of the selection, which can then be pasted. To copy a picture, or a part of it, and paste it in another part of the picture, follow the steps given below:

1. Select the part of the drawing you want to copy by using the **Select** tool in the **Image** group.
2. Click on the **Copy** option in the **Clipboard** group.

Fig. 5.5 | *Copying and pasting an image*

3. Click on the **Paste** option in the **Clipboard** group.
4. With the picture still selected, move it to a new location in the Drawing Area.

Soak up!

The cut/copied part of the picture is stored in a temporary folder called Clipboard.

Crank up!

Technology Literacy

Some important keyboard shortcuts used in MS Paint 2016 are given below:

Action	Keyboard Shortcut
To select the entire picture	Ctrl+A
To cut a part of the picture	Ctrl+X
To copy a part of the picture	Ctrl+C
To paste the cut/copied part of the picture	Ctrl+V

Brush up!

Draw two yellow circles in MS Paint. Copy these circles and paste them on the drawing area. Now, using the **Selection** tool, select the second one and change its colour, as shown below.

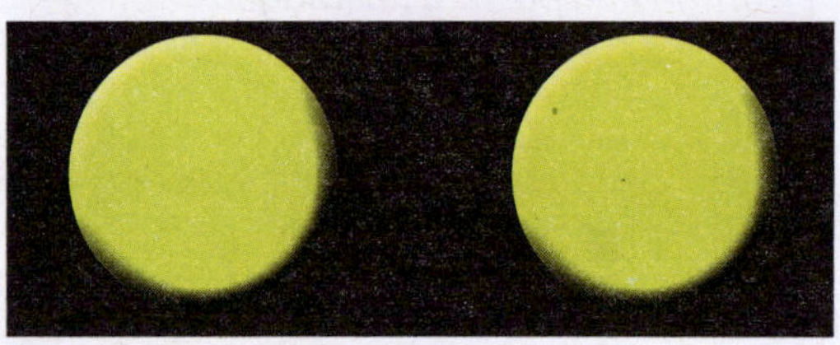

Image Group

The **Image** group consists of four tools: Select, Crop, Rotate and Resize. We have learned how to use the **Select** tool. Let us discuss the other tools in detail.

Soak up!

Cropped images from one drawing can be copied and pasted in another drawing.

Cropping an Image

The **Crop tool** is used to select an area of the picture and cut out everything outside that area.

To use this tool, follow the steps given below:

1. Using the **Select** tool, select the part of the image you want to keep.
2. Click on the **Crop** tool in the Image group. You will see that only the cropped part of the image remains on the drawing area (Fig. 5.6).

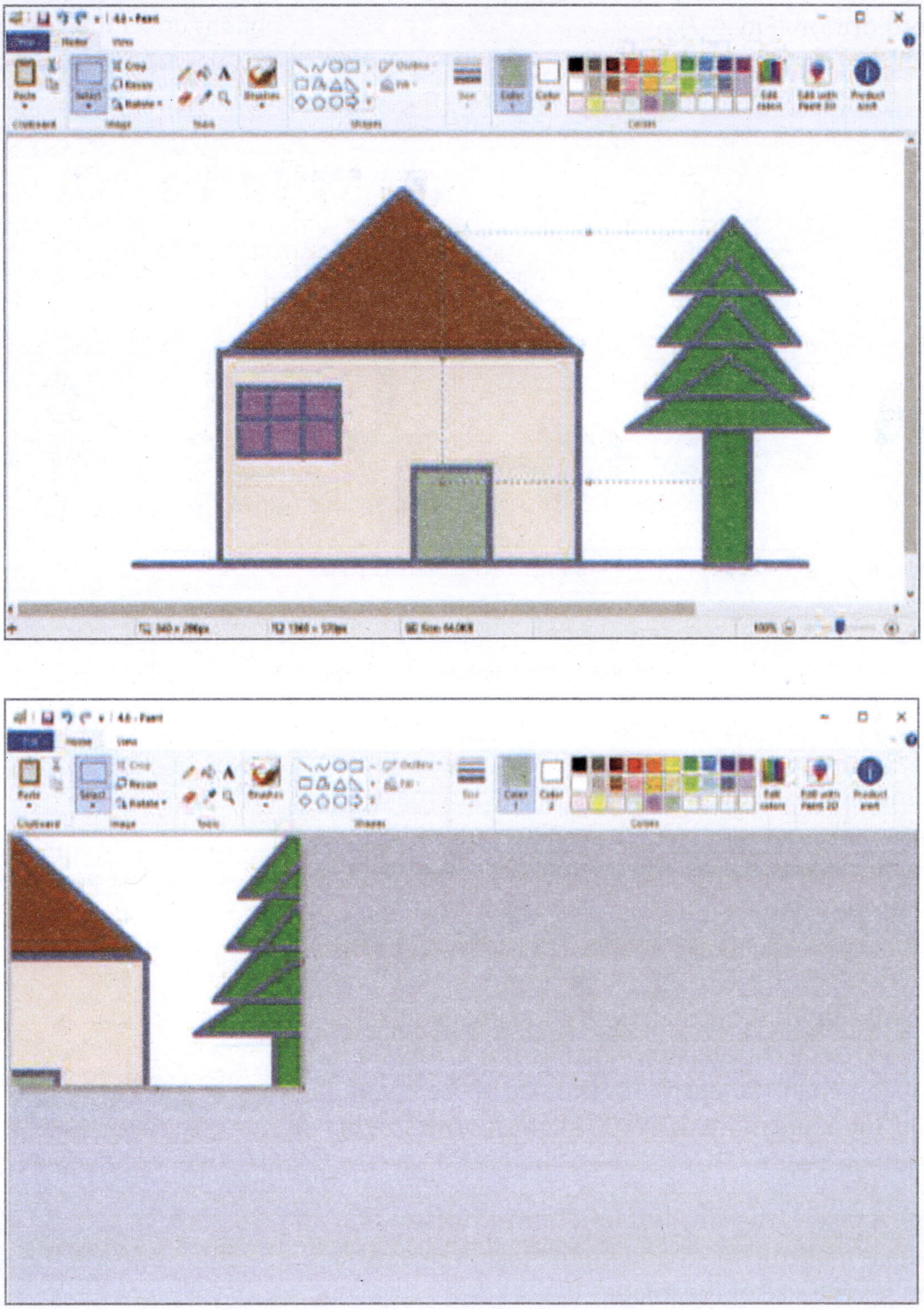

Fig. 5.6 | *Using the Crop tool*

Rotating an Image

The **Rotate** tool is used to turn the image to point in any direction, such as up, down, left or right. To use the **Rotate** tool, select the picture, click on the **Rotate** tool in the **Image** group and then select the desired option (Fig. 5.7).

Clear up!

Draw an image of a bird in MS Paint. Now, explore the various options under the Rotate tool.

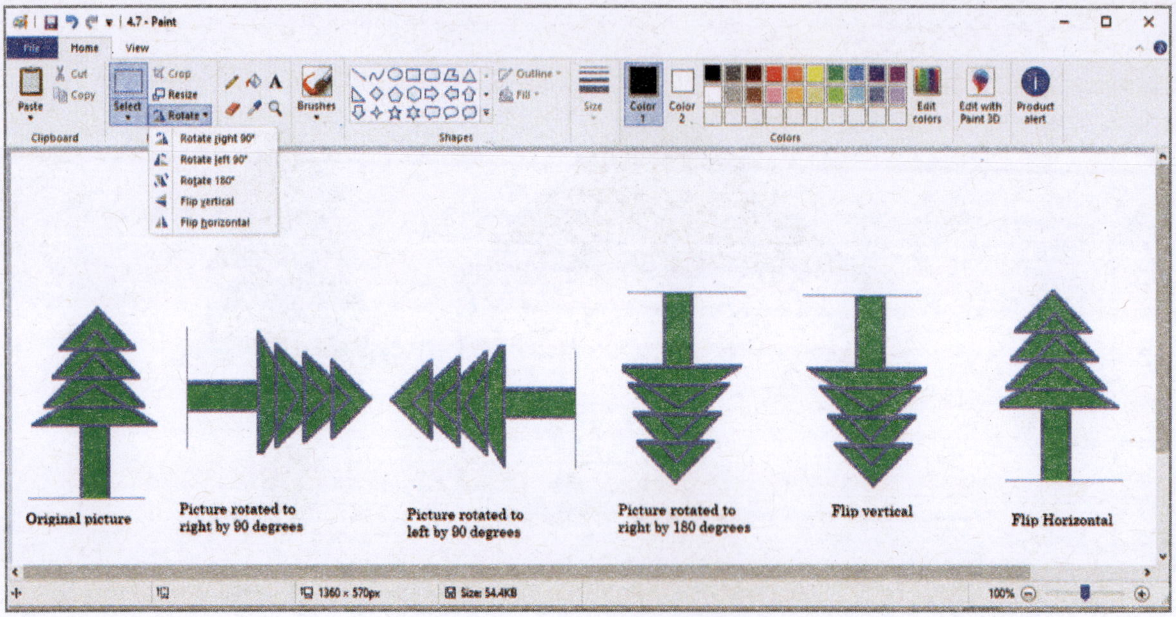

Fig. 5.7 | *Using the Rotate tool*

Resizing the Image

As the name suggests, the **Resize** tool is used to make the image smaller or bigger. When we click on this tool, the **Resize and Skew** dialog box opens up, as shown in Fig. 5.8. It gives us options to resize and skew the image.

The image can be resized by:

- **Percentage**: This is used to resize the image in relation to the current size, which is 100%. Any value less than 100 decreases the size of the image, while any value more than 100 increases the size of the image.
- **Pixel**: A pixel is the smallest unit from which an image is made up of. Changing the pixel values also changes the size of the image.

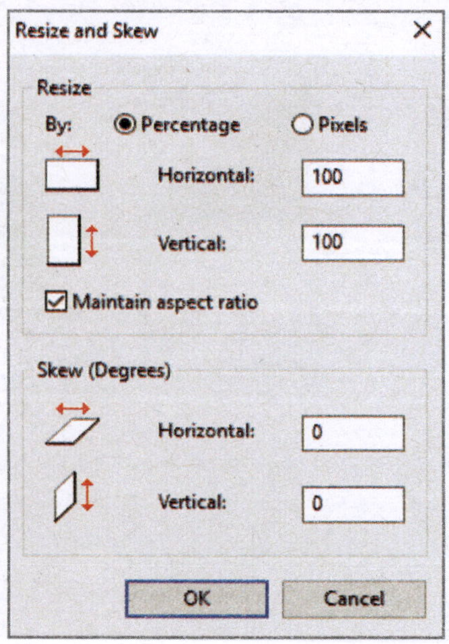

Fig. 5.8 | *Resize and Skew dialog box*

Figure 5.9 shows a resized picture.

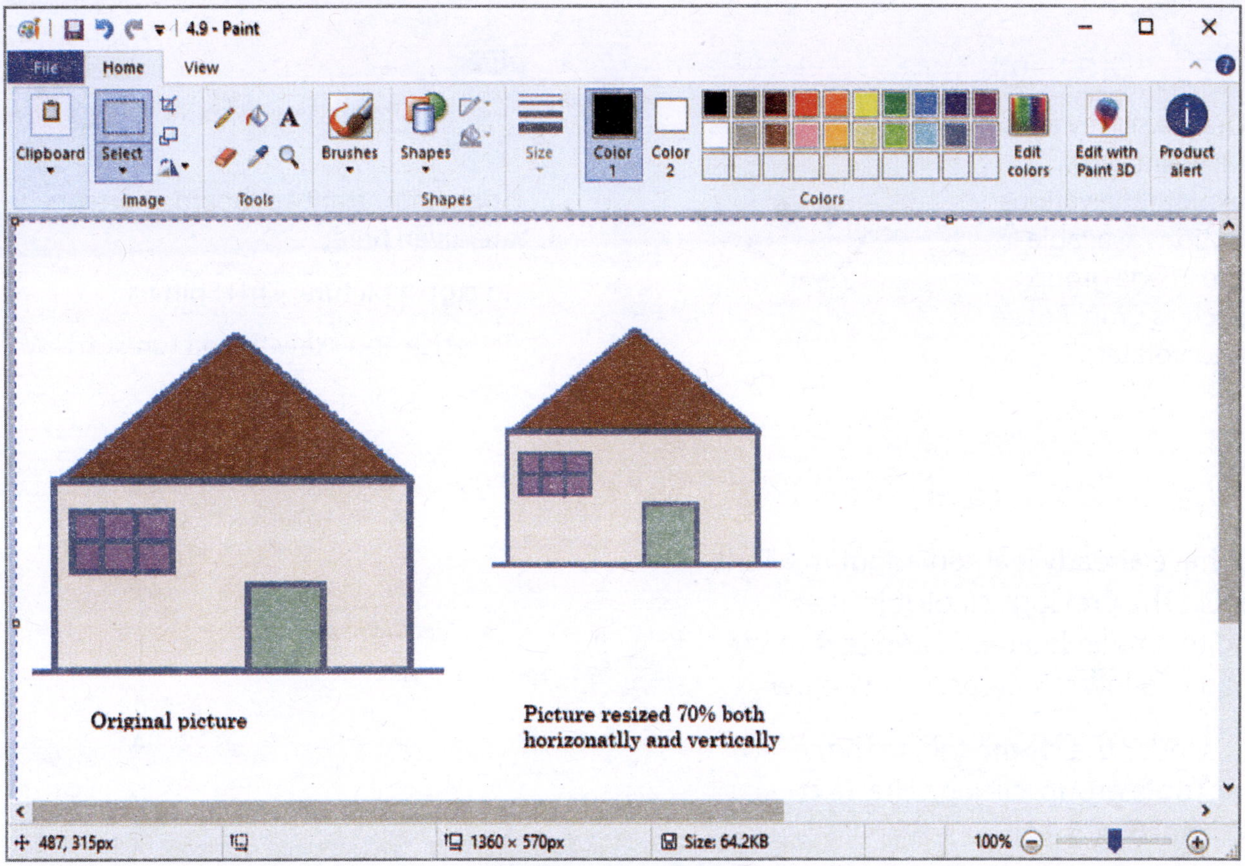

Fig. 5.9 | *Resized picture*

Similarly, to skew (tilt) the image, enter the numbers in the Horizontal and Vertical boxes (Fig. 5.10).

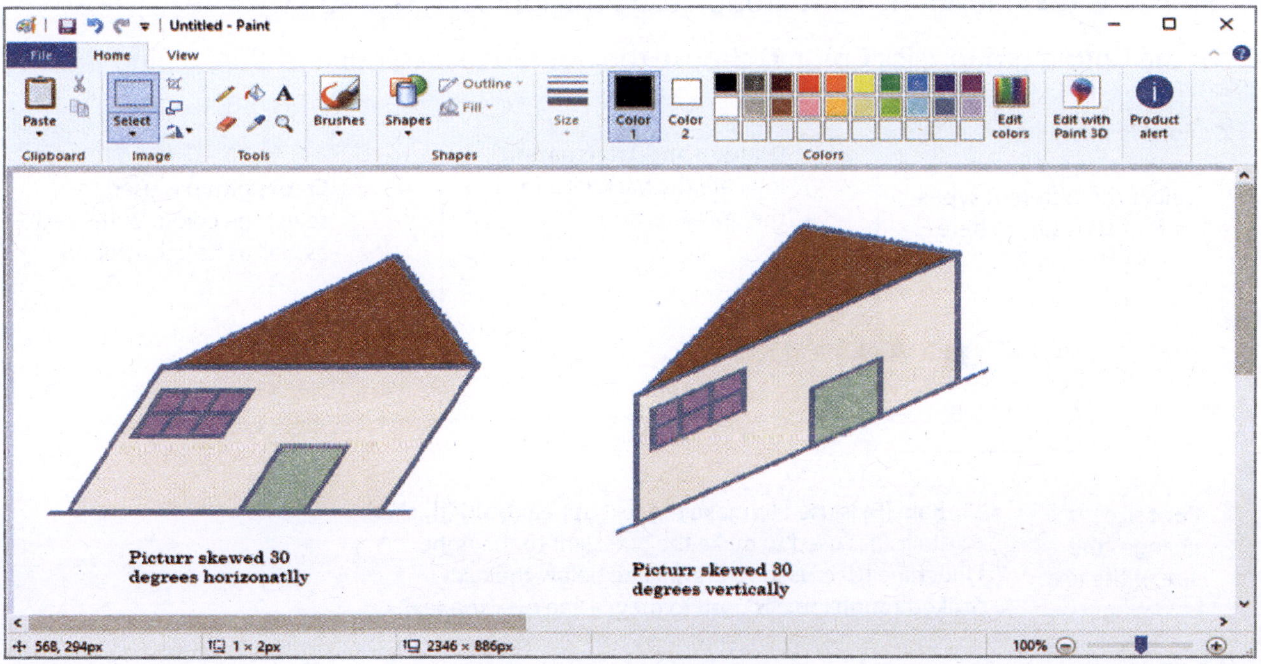

Fig. 5.10 | *Skewed pictures*

Clear up!

Draw a smiley in MS Paint. Now, explore the various options available in the Image group, such as Crop, Resize and Rotate.

Technology Literacy

Crank up!

Some important keyboard shortcuts are given here:

To crop a picture: Ctrl+Shift+X

To resize and skew the picture: Ctrl+W

More on the Text Tool

We have already learned about the **Text** tool in the previous class. It is used to add text to an image. To add text to the image, follow the steps given below:

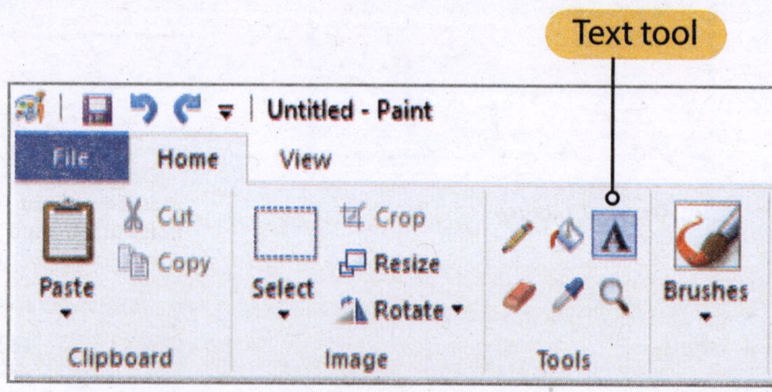

Fig. 5.11 | *Text tool*

1. Under the **Home** tab, in the **Tools** group, click on the **Text** tool (Fig. 5.11).
2. Drag the pointer to the drawing area where the text needs to be added. Notice that the Text tab appears on the Paint window (Fig. 5.12).
3. From the **Text** tab, in the **Font** group, select the font face, size and style.
4. In the **Colors** group, click **Color 1**, choose the desired text colour and start typing the text.

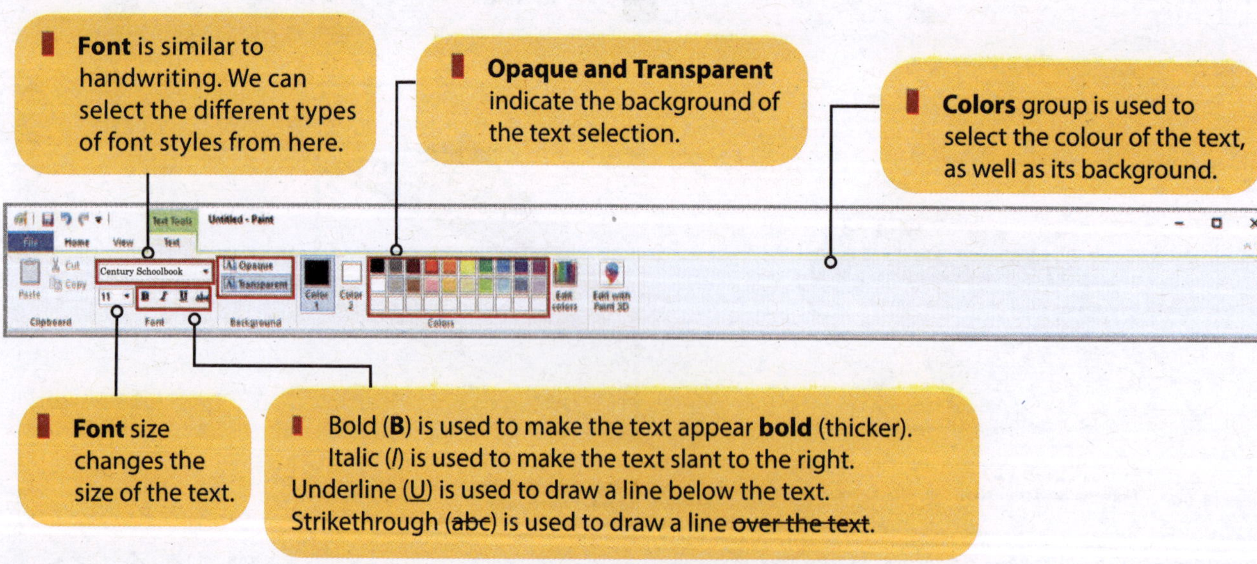

Fig. 5.12 | *Text tab*

Other Useful Tools in MS Paint

Callouts

MS Paint gives the option of shapes to draw the commonly used ones. These include shapes, such as circle, semicircle, sqaure, rectangle, triangle and even callouts. Callouts are used to label parts of an image or used to represent a conversation. We can insert a callout in similar to the way in which we insert shapes in our drawings. The three types of callouts are shown in Fig. 5.13.

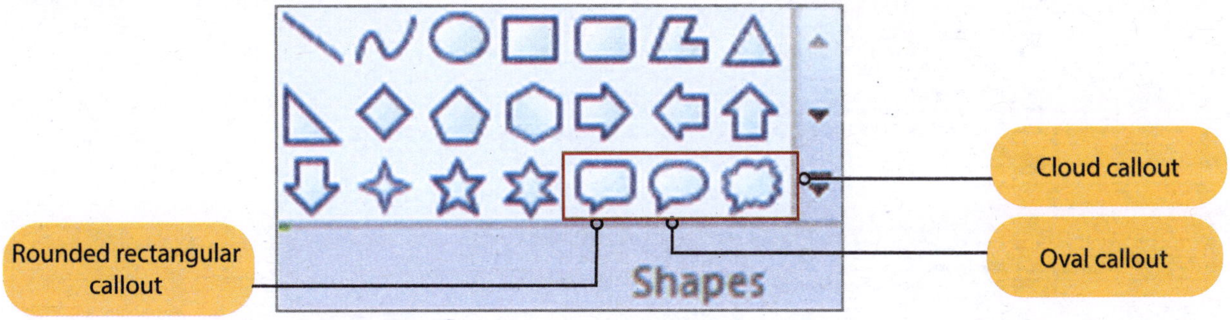

Fig. 5.13 | *Types of callouts*

Color Picker

The Color picker tool is used to copy colour from one part of the picture and fill another part with the same colour. To use this tool:

1. Click on the **Color picker** tool from the **Tools** group (Fig. 5.14).
2. Click on the part of the picture from where you want to pick the colour. The picked-up colour will be reflected as **Color 1**.
3. Move the mouse pointer to the part of the picture where you want to apply the same colour. Then, click on it once to apply the same colour.

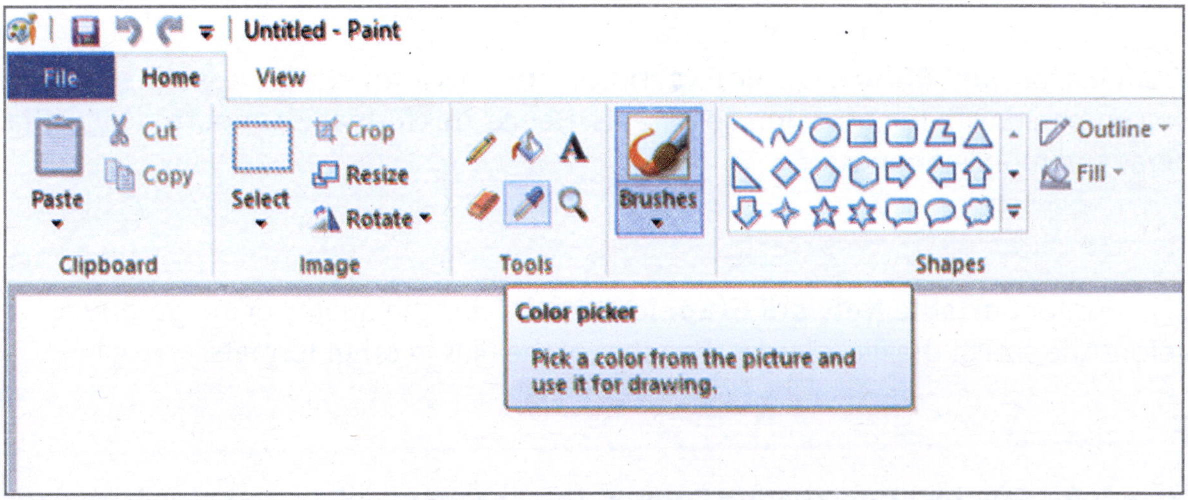

Fig. 5.14 | *Color picker tool*

File Formats

When we save a file, we write its name in the **File name** box. Later, we can access the file with this name. Notice the **Save as type** box in Fig. 5.16. It shows the type of image as PNG (*.png). Here, .png is the extension used to save the file. It is also known as the file format.

We can change the file format by clicking the drop-down arrow and selecting a file format to save the file.

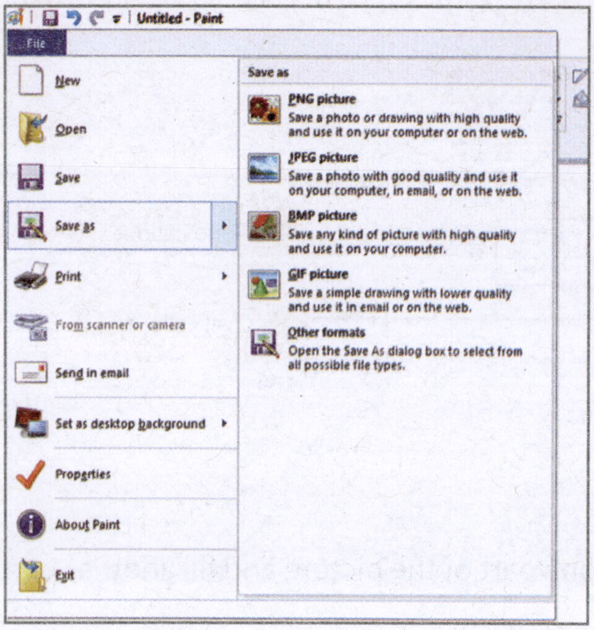

Fig. 5.15 | *Different file extensions while saving an image*

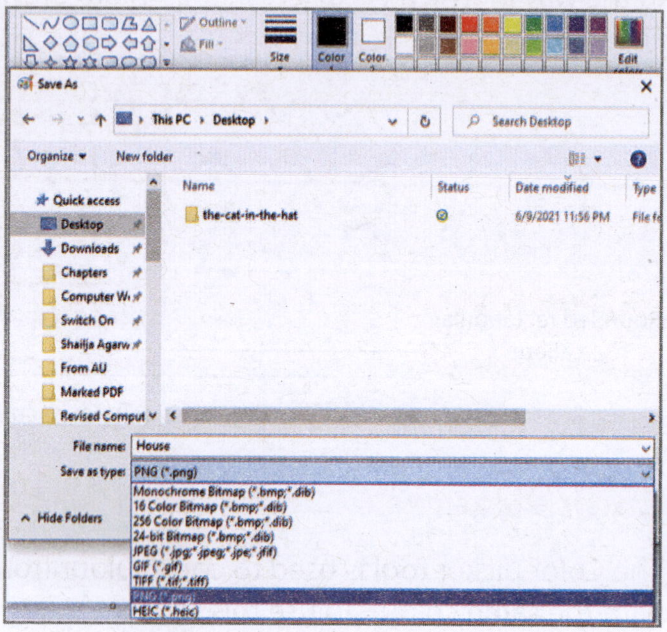

Fig. 5.16 | *File extensions while saving a picture*

The different image files have different file formats, such as .jpeg, .png and .gif. This means that the images are saved in different formats.

Some of the commonly used image formats are discussed here:

JPEG

JPEG stands for **Joint Photographic Experts Group**. This format takes less storage space when compared with the other image formats. Hence, this format is supported by digital cameras and mobile phones.

PNG

PNG stands for **Portable Network Graphics**. It maintains the quality of image, and therefore, the size of the file is larger than that of the files in other formats.

GIF

GIF stands for **Graphics Interchange Format**. This image format are commonly used for drawing cartoons and animations.

Clear up!

Take your teacher's help to search a picture of your school. Open it using MS Paint. Now, add your school's name on it using Times New Roman font in size 20 and in blue colour.

Soak up!

MS Paint allows us to create 3D drawing as well. When we click on the Edit with Paint 3D option on the MS Paint window, a new window appears, which allows us to create 3D paintings.

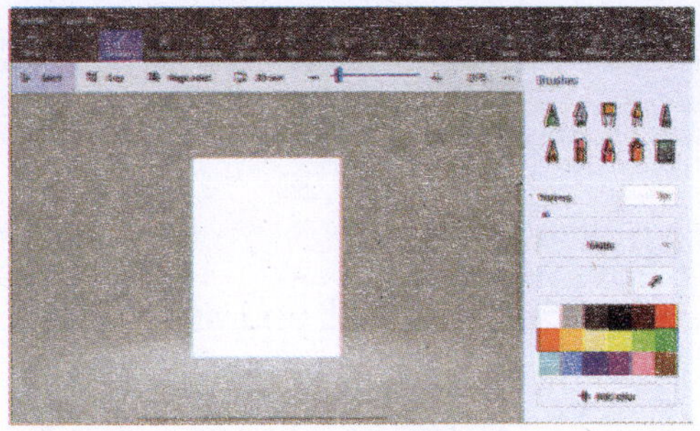

Today I learned!

- The Selection group tools can be used to select parts of a picture in various shapes.
- The Clipboard group has the Cut, Copy and Paste tools.
- The Image group has various tools, which help us crop, rotate and resize images.
- The Tools group offers various tools such as the Pencil and Text tool, which helps us write on an image.
- Rectangular selection is used to select a square or a rectangular part of a picture.
- Free-form selection is used to select an irregularly-shaped part of a picture.
- Cut and Paste commands are used to remove or delete a picture, or a part of a picture, and paste it in another place on the drawing area.
- Copy and Paste options are used to duplicate or copy a picture, or a part of a picture, and paste it in another place on the drawing area.
- The Crop tool is used to select an area of the picture and cut out everything outside that area.
- The Rotate tool is used to rotate or flip a picture or a part of a picture.
- The Resize tool is used to resize or skew a picture or a part of a picture.
- The Text tool is used to type text.
- .jpeg and .png are some of the formats in which MS Paint files are saved.

Revise and polish!

1. Tick (✓) the correct answer.

a. Which of these tools is used to go back on the last action performed?

(i) Flip ☐	(ii) Undo ☐
(iii) Redo ☐	(iv) Rotate ☐

b. Which tool will you use to cut out one portion of a drawing?

(i) Cut ☐	(ii) Crop ☐
(iii) Copy ☐	(iv) Resize ☐

c. Which tool is used to change the size of the image?

(i) Select ☐	(ii) Group ☐
(iii) All ☐	(iv) Resize ☐

d. Which of these groups will you use to change the colour of the drawing?

(i) Font type ☐	(ii) Colors ☐
(iii) Size ☐	(iv) Align ☐

e. Which of the following is a format in which a MS Paint file can be saved as an image?

(i) .jpeg ☐	(ii) .doc ☐
(iii) .xls ☐	(iv) .pdf ☐

2. Fill in the blanks using the given words.

Rotate Pixel Ctrl+C Color Picker draw

a. MS Paint is an application used to __________ on the computer.

b. The __________ allows the user to pick any color in an image on the screen.

c. __________ is the smallest unit from which an image is made up of.

d. __________ is used to turn the image to point in any direction, such as up, down, left or right.

e. __________ is the keyboard shortcut for copying the image.

3. Match the following.

a.		(i)	Crop
b.		(ii)	Paste
c.		(iii)	Select
d.		(iv)	Rotate

4. Write the keyboard shortcuts for the following commands.

a. Cut ____________________

b. Copy ____________________

c. Paste ____________________

d. Select all ____________________

e. Crop ____________________

Experiential Learning

Lab Activities

1. Draw the following pictures by using the various tools in MS Paint:

   a. Flower   b. Book

   c. Candy   d. Dice

2. Look at the following picture of seven days of the week. Choose a day of your choice and paste (draw) it in the blank area. Colour the day using the your favourite colours. Can you do this in MS Paint? Name the tools you will be using for this.

3. Guess the names of the following objects. Now, using the Text tool, write their names in MS Paint in the styles given below:

S. No.	Image	Font Style	Font Colour
a.		Calibri, Size: 30, Bold, Underline and Transparent	Brown
b.		Comic Sans MS, Size: 45, Bold, Underline, Opaque with white background	Purple

4. Sameer and Rima decided to draw a scenery by dividing it into two parts. Now, they are unable to join both the drawings together to make it into a big scenery. Which MS Paint tools should they use for it?

5. Using Shapes and Text tools in MS Paint, show how to do simple additions and subtractions.

Hint: You can draw vertical lines as you do on your notebook while adding or subtracting.

Chapter 6

File Management

After reading this chapter, I will be able to:

- ✔ Define files and folders.
- ✔ Understand about File Explorer in Windows 10.
- ✔ Discuss how to create a file and a folder.
- ✔ Understand how to close and open a file and a folder.

Life Skills

Brainstorm and explore!

Where will you store the following objects?

1. 	a. 
2. 	b. 
3. 	c. 
4. 	d. 

Look at this figure. Do you think you will be able to find your crayons and colouring book in this mess?

____

We have learned about files in the previous class. A file is an object that stores data and information. It is recognized by its extension.

In this chapter, we will learn about folders.

Fig. 6.1 | *A messy room*

Folders

We keep crayons in the crayon box and keep the crayon box in the drawer (Fig. 6.2). Unless we keep our things organized, it will be difficult for us to find them.

organizing: the process of arranging things in an orderly manner

Fig. 6.2 | *Keeping things organized*

Likewise, we should store all our data in a computer neatly. Well-organized data is easy to find. Data is stored in a computer using files and folders.

Fig. 6.3 | *Organizing data in a computer*

If we compare Figs. 6.2 and 6.3, we will see that the crayon is same as data, the crayon box is same as a file, and the drawer is the same as a folder.

A **folder** is a container where many files can be stored. Folders can also store other folders. A folder within a folder is called a **subfolder**. A folder helps organize files on a computer.

Clear up!

What do these files store? Match the columns.

1. .jpeg	a. Music video
2. .mp4	b. Essay on my computer
3. .doc	c. My birthday picture

File Explorer in Windows 10

We have learned how to keep our things neatly. For example, we keep our pencils in a pencil box, and then we put the pencil box in a cupboard. The cupboard too is kept in a particular room. Similarly, all folders and files are stored in **drives** on a computer. A computer can have more than one drive. Figure 6.4 shows the various drives on a Windows 10 computer (In this case, there are drives from C to H).

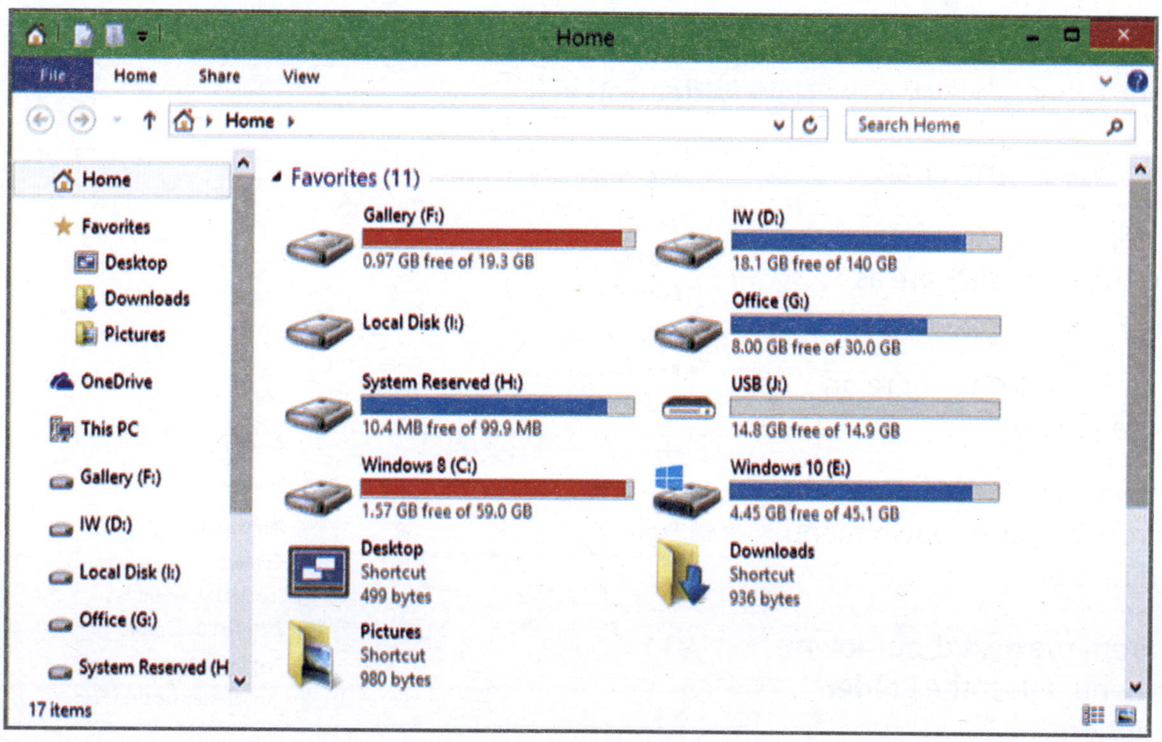

Fig. 6.4 | *Different drives on a computer*

The File Explorer shows us the different drives on our computer. There are three ways to open it:

- Click on the **Start** → **Windows System** → **File Explorer**, as shown in Fig. 6.5.

Or

- Double-click on the **This PC** icon  This PC on the desktop.

Or

- Press **Windows** () and E keys together on the keyboard.

desktop: the main screen area after we turn on the computer

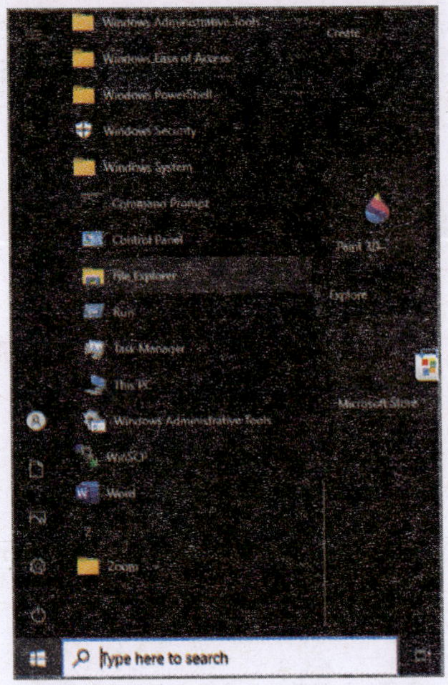

Fig. 6.5 | *Opening File Explorer*

Creating Files and Folders in Windows 10

We already know that we can organize data into folders and subfolders. The contents of a file/folder can be viewed by double-clicking on it. Let us learn how to create a folder/file in Windows 10.

Creating a Folder

There are two ways to create a folder: one is by right-clicking anywhere on the screen and the other is by using the **New folder** option.

Using the Right-click

The steps to create a folder using the right-click are as follows:

1. Right-click anywhere on the screen.
2. Select the **New** option from the drop-down menu (Fig. 6.6).
3. From the next drop-down menu, select the **Folder** option.

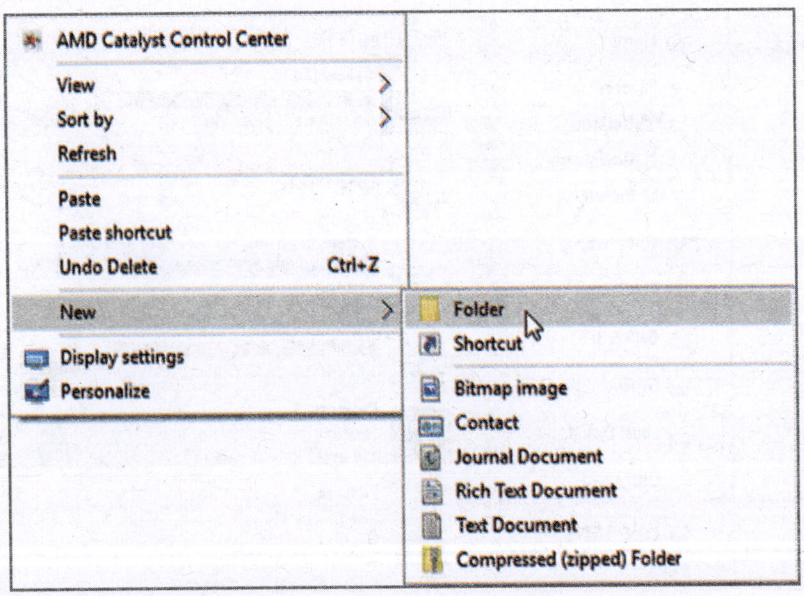

Fig. 6.6 | *Creating a new folder using the right-click*

Using the New Folder Option

The steps for creating a subfolder inside a folder are as follows:

1. Select the folder in which you want a new folder.
2. Click on the **New folder** option, as shown in Fig. 6.7.

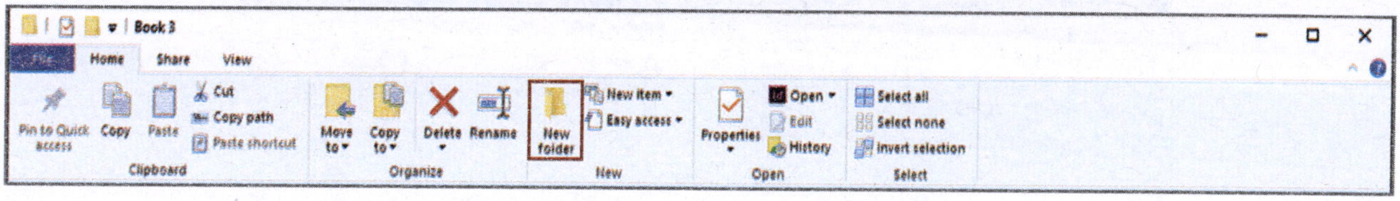

Fig. 6.7 | *Using the New folder option*

A new folder will be created on the desktop or in the selected folder, as shown in Fig. 6.8.

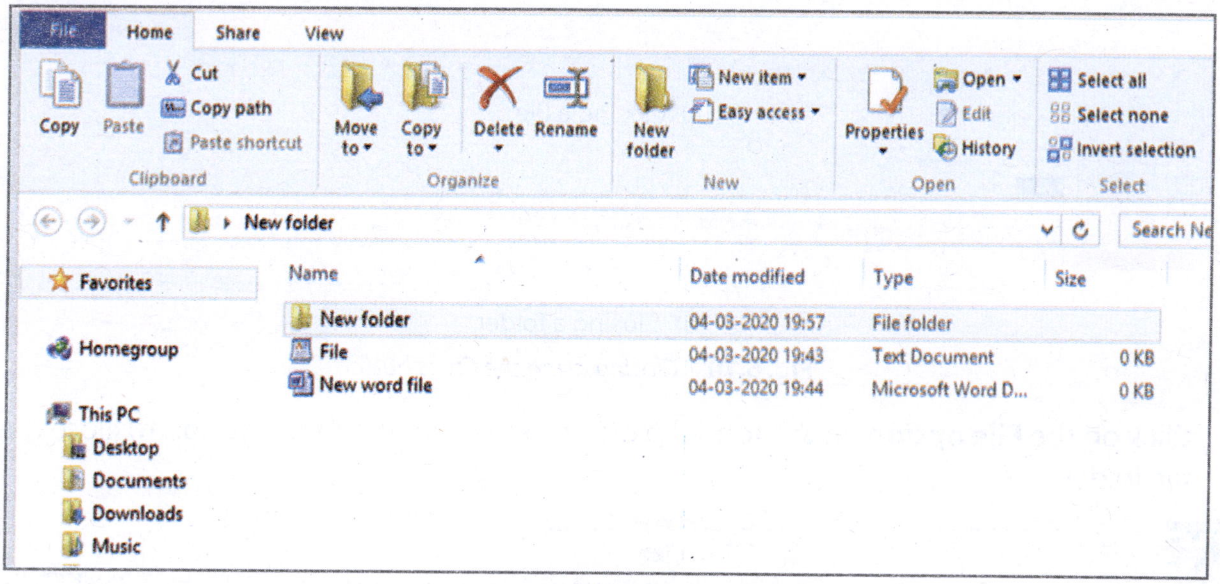

Fig. 6.8 | *New folder created*

Creating a File

A file is created in a similar manner. To create a text file, right-click anywhere on the screen, select → **New** → **Text Document**, as shown in Fig. 6.9.

To create a file inside a specific folder, open the folder. Then, follow the same steps used for creating a file on the desktop.

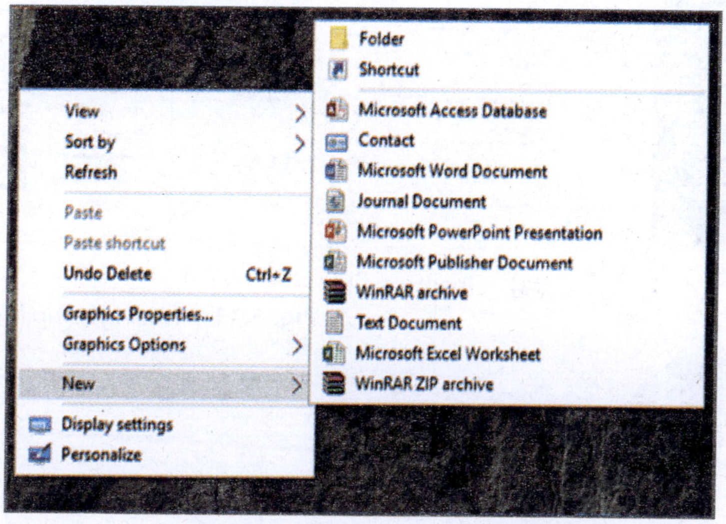

Fig. 6.9 | *Creating a new text file*

Closing a File/Folder

There are two ways to close a file/folder.

1. Just like any other program, click on the × on the top right of the file/folder.

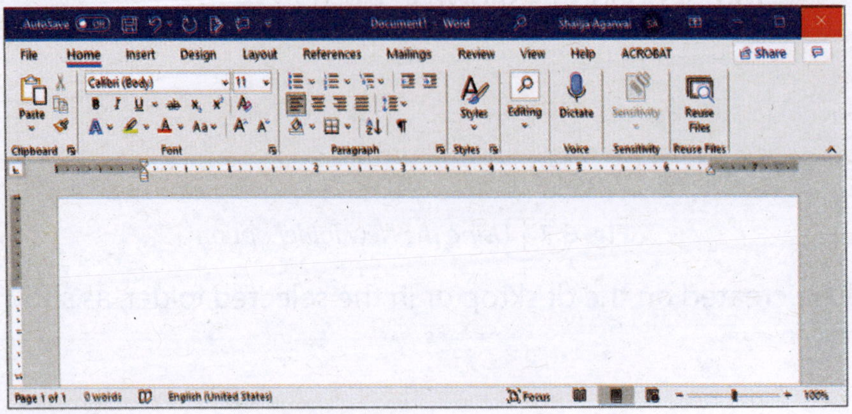

(a) Closing a file

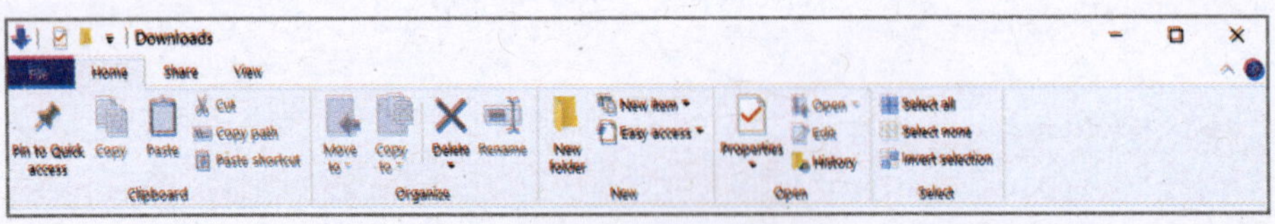

(b) Closing a folder

Fig. 6.10 | *Closing using the Cross button*

2. Click on the **File option** on the top-left corner → Click on the **Close** option to close the file folder.

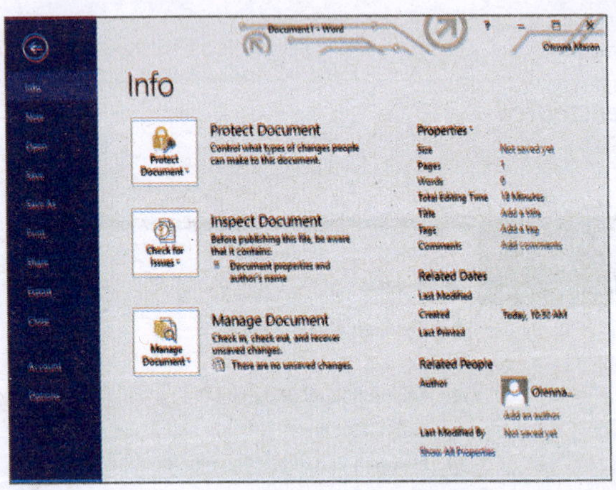

(a) Closing a file

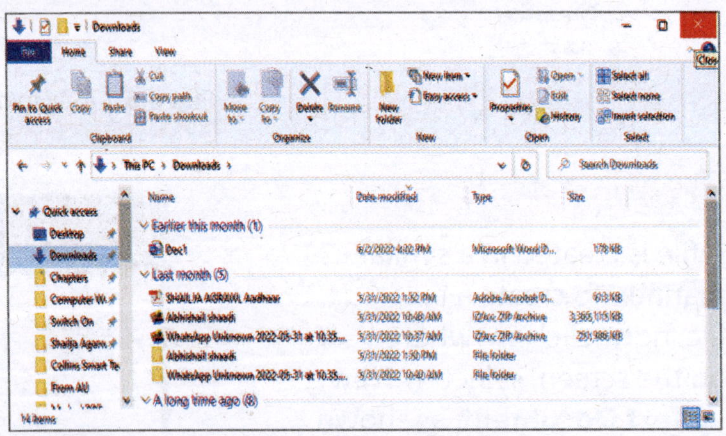

(b) Closing a folder

Fig. 6.11 | *Closing using the File option*

Soak up!

Remember to always save the file before closing it; else, you will lose the content in it.

Opening an Already Saved File/Folder

To open an already saved file or folder, simply move the mouse pointer on the particular folder/file icon and double-click using the mouse (Fig. 6.12).

Brush up!

We know one way to open a file or folder is to double-click on the icon with the mouse. Can you tell any other way?

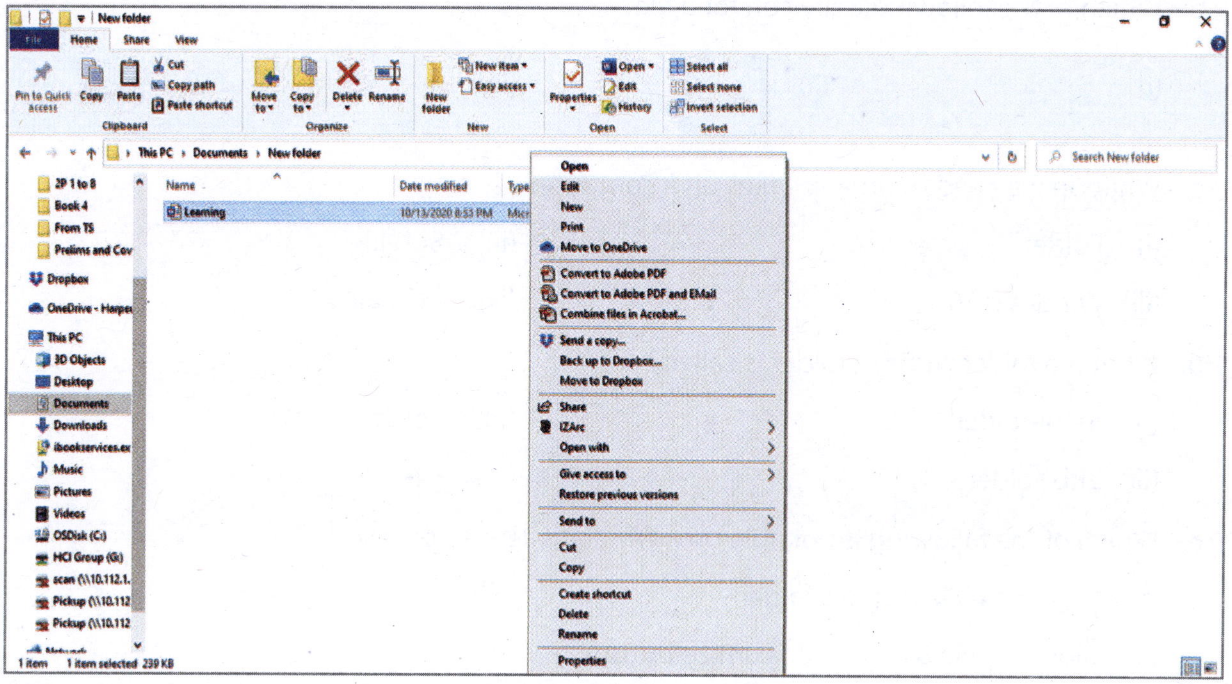

Fig. 6.12 | *Opening a document*

Today I learned!

- We should always store all the data in a computer neatly, using files and folders, so that they are easy to find later.
- A file stores data and information, while a folder organizes the files in a group.
- A folder is a container to store many files.
- The File Explorer shows us drives on our computer.
- There are multiple ways of creating a file or folder on a Windows 10 computer.
- There are two ways to close a file/folder.
- We can open an already saved file or folder by simple double-clicking on its icon.

Revise and polish!

1. Tick (✓) the correct answer.

a. Which of the following is an icon for a folder?

(i)  ☐ (ii)  ☐ (iii)  ☐ (iv)  ☐

b. Which of the following is an icon for a file?

(i)  ☐ (ii)  ☐ (iii)  ☐ (iv)  ☐

c. What do we need to organize files on a computer?

(i) Folder ☐ (ii) Sub file ☐

(iii) Windows 10 ☐ (iv) MS Paint ☐

d. What is a folder within a folder is called?

(i) Semi-folder ☐ (ii) Folder ☐

(iii) Sub-folder ☐ (iv) File ☐

e. Which of the following is possible on a Windows 10 computer?

(i) Creating a file inside a folder ☐

(ii) Closing a file using the Maximize button ☐

(iii) Deleting a folder using the Close button ☐

(iv) Organizing files using the Paint application ☐

2. Spot the differences between a file and a folder and complete the following table.

same formats files many information one

File		Folder	
a.	A file stores ________.	b.	A folder organizes ________ on a computer.
c.	There are ________ types of files.	d.	Folders can be created in just ________ way.
e.	Files have different file ________, depending on the kind of information stored.	f.	Folders remain the ________.

3. Fill in the blanks using the given words.

save   Text Document   folders   Organizing   mouse

a. To create a new text file on the desktop, click on New → ____________.

b. One should always ____________ the file before closing it.

c. To open a particular folder, double-click on it using a ____________.

d. ____________ is the process of arranging things neatly.

e. We should always store all the data in a computer neatly, using files and____________.

4. State whether the following statements are true (T) or false (F).

a. The new file option can be used to create a sub-folder. ☐

b. To open a file, we need to double-click on its icon. ☐

c. Folder within a folder is called a file. ☐

d. All folders are stored in drives in a computer. ☐

e. A file is used to organize data on a computer. ☐

5. Answer the following questions in brief.

a. Define a folder.

b. Why do we need to organize data in a computer? Explain with examples.

c. Draw the icon of a folder.

d. What are the two ways to create a folder?

e. Explain how to close a folder.

Lab Activities

1. Go to the computer lab and create a new folder on the desktop. Draw the icon for the same in the given space.

2. Create a new MS Word file inside the new folder. Write five lines about your mother in that file. Save the file as mother.docx and close it. Re-open it to see if it was saved properly and has the correct data.

3. Varun just got a new computer. He has different files and folders from his older computer that he needs to move to the new one using a pen drive. Look at the following icons and help him organize them.

a.	 Computer Homework.docx	(i)	 Music
b.	 Song.mp3	(ii)	 Homework
c.	 Inside Out.mp4	(iii)	 Photos
d.	 Cakecutting.jpg	(iv)	 Movies
e.	 English Project.docx	(v)	 My B'day pics

Think and Answer

1. Mrunal has been typing a three-page essay using MS Word. She finished it last night before shutting down the computer. When she reopened the file today, she did not find the work she had typed last night. What happened to the typed matter?

2. Shweta and Aditya share the same computer and have multiple files on the desktop. Both if them find it difficult to locate the required file. Can you help them find their files quickly?

Worksheet 1 (Chapters 1 and 2)

1. Solve the following crossword using the hints given below.

DOWN

1. Paint is an __________ software used to draw and save pictures on a computer.
2. I resemble a TV.
3. I am a hardware device used to right-click on computer objects to open a menu screen.
4. The bar at the bottom of the desktop screen.

ACROSS

5. I help the computer to make mathematical decisions.
6. I can quickly show all the open windows on the desktop.
7. I can input a physical photograph on the computer screen.
8. I help to get a printout from the computer.

2. Answer the following questions.

a. Saloni needs to submit an assignment to her teacher. She needs to add pictures to the assignment. She has taken the pictures from the internet. Which part of the computer will she use to take the hardcopies of these pictures?

____

b. Smita attends classes online and needs to write an essay to pass the class test. Which device will help her to type in the computer?

____

c. Ishan wants to play music on his computer. Which device does he need to connect to the computer for this?

____

d. After 10 pm, Ishan needs to lower the volume on his computer. From where can he change the settings?

____

3. Look at the pictures of machines given below and fill in the blanks.

	Machine	Input	Process	Output
a.		Pressing numbers and symbols		Calculated answer
b.		Switching on the fan	Fan blades rotating rapidly	
c.		Selecting the power		Baked food
d.			Washing	Clean clothes

4. Solve the following problems and fill in the blanks.

	Input	Process	Output
a.	4, 5, +	4 + 5	
b.	*, 2, 7		14
c.		9 / 3	

Worksheet 2 (Chapters 3 and 4)

1. **Draw the symbols used to represent the following tabs/tools.**

   a. Cut b. Undo c. Web browser of your choice

2. **Divya is typing an essay on the topic 'My favourite animal' in an MS Word document.**

   a. Can you help her with the steps on how to open MS Word?

   ____

   ____

   b. Her mouse is not working and she has access to the keyboard only. Do you think it is possible to still complete the assignment? If yes, how so?

   ____

   ____

3. **Answer the following questions in one word.**

   a. Name the tab used to close the window of MS Word. ____________

   b. Name the group that has Copy and Paste options in MS Word. ____________

4. **Give the full form of the following.**

   a. MS Word ____________

   b. URL ____________

   c. WWW ____________

5. **Search on the internet and find out the capitals of the following countries.**

   a. France ____________

   b. India ____________

   c. Sri Lanka ____________

   d. USA ____________

   e. Germany ____________

6. **Tick (✓) the activities you have done using the internet.**

a. Send emails ☐

b. Play games ☐

c. Use social media ☐

d. Video call with friends ☐

e. Download software ☐

f. Shop from an online store ☐

7. **Cross (✗) the unsafe activities on the internet.**

a. Share password with your best friend so they can help you when you forget. ☐

b. Write down your password at the back of your notebook. ☐

c. Shop from http://www.xyzshop.com. ☐

d. Click on the popup that says you have been chosen to win a lottery of 100000$. ☐

e. Share contact information with strangers you have met on gaming sites. ☐

f. Set the password to 123456 so that you will never forget it. ☐

8. **Write a poem in six line. Type it using MS Word.**

Worksheet 3 (Chapters 5 and 6)

Learning Skills

1. Do you know the logos/icons of the following companies? If yes, draw them using MS Paint. Name the tools used to draw these.

a. Mercedes

b. Pepsi

c. Olympic

d. YouTube

e. Pokemon Ball

2. Gautam has created a word file "My favourite sport" in the D drive on a computer with Windows 10 operating system. Can you help him find and open it? Write down the steps to do so.

____

____

____

____

3. Give steps to do the following activities.

a. Create a folder "My projects" on your computer.

b. Inside the folder, make two folders named 'Projects in MS Paint' and 'Projects in MS Word'.

c. Now, copy all the saved drawings in the 'Projects in MS Paint' folder.

d. Create a new text file to write an essay on how to stay safe online. What name did you use to save the file? ____________

e. Close the file and reopen it.

____

____

____

____

____

____

4. Draw the following images using MS Paint. Remember to save it in the "Projects in MS Paint" folder.

Competency-based question

a. Car

b. Ice cream cone

c. House

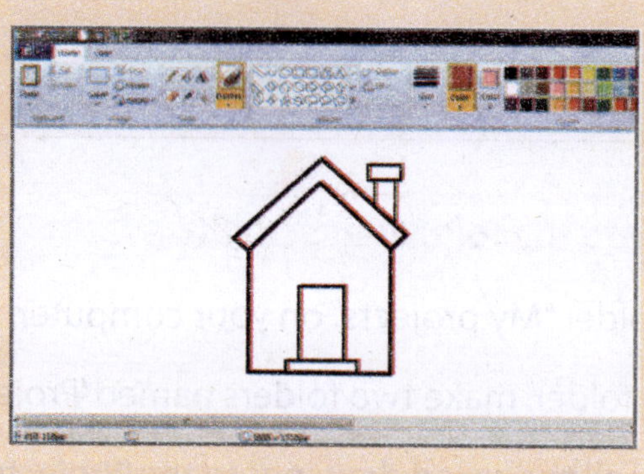

d. Folder

Additional Worksheet

1. Fill in the blank spaces with the correct alphabets or numbers.

a.	Fill in the missing letters for the word that means the following. A stream of water running into the sea (plural).	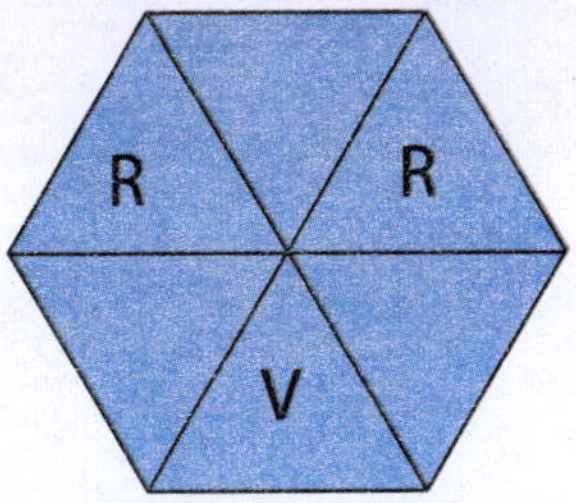
b.	Fill in the missing numbers that will add up the numbers in the hexagon to 30.	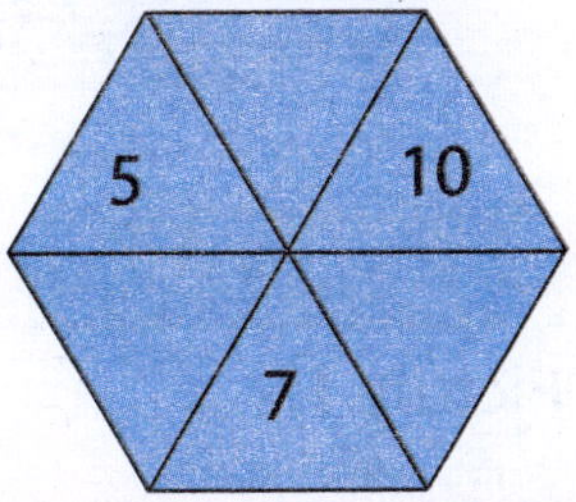

2. Create patterns from the given shapes. Create as many as possible from the given ones!

a. 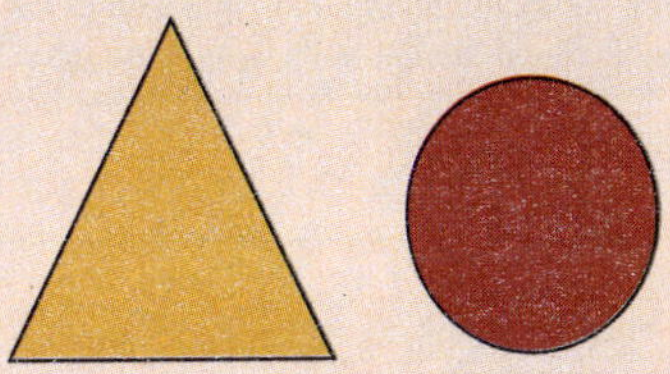

b. 

3. Create two drawings using the following shapes. This could be an object or even a scenery. Use each element as many times as required. Be creative with both colours and sizes!

Picture 1:

Picture 2:

Fun Activity

Colour the following pixels to reveal the secret image.

Red colour: 2D, 2G, 3E, 3F, 5D, 5G, 7E, 8G, 9D, 9G

Black colour: 4D, 4E, 4F, 4G, 5C, 5E, 5F, 5H, 6B, 6C, 6D, 6E, 6F, 6G, 6H, 6I, 7B, 7C, 7D, 7F, 7G, 7H, 7I, 8B, 8C, 8D, 8E, 8F, 8H, 8I, 9C, 9E, 9F, 9H,10D, 10E, 10F, 10G

	A	B	C	D	E	F	G	H	I	J
1										
2										
3										
4										
5										
6										
7										
8										
9										
10										

CLASS 3

QUESTION PAPER SET A

NCO

SOF NATIONAL CYBER OLYMPIAD 2021-22

DO NOT OPEN THIS BOOKLET UNTIL ASKED TO DO SO

Total Questions: 35 | Time: 1 hr.

Guidelines for the Candidate

1. You will get additional ten minutes to fill up information about yourself on the OMR Sheet, before the start of the exam.
2. Write your **Name, School Code, Class, Roll No.** and **Mobile Number** clearly on the **OMR Sheet** and do not forget to sign it. We will share your marks / result and other information related to SOF exams on your mobile number.
3. The Question Paper comprises three sections:

   Logical Reasoning (5 Questions), **Computers and Information Technology** (25 Questions) and **Achievers Section** (5 Questions).

   Each question in Achievers Section carries 2 marks, whereas all other questions carry one mark each.
4. All questions are compulsory. There is no negative marking. Use of calculator is not permitted.
5. There is only ONE correct answer. Choose only ONE option for an answer.
6. To mark your choice of answers by darkening the circles on the OMR Sheet, use **HB Pencil** or **Blue / Black ball point pen** only. E.g.

   Q.16: _____ means to hold down the left mouse button while you move the mouse pointer to a new place.

   A. Single click B. Double click C. Dragging D. Left click

   As the correct answer is option C, you must darken the circle corresponding to option C on the OMR Sheet. 16. Ⓐ Ⓑ ● Ⓓ
7. Rough work should be done in the blank space provided in this booklet.
8. Return the OMR Sheet to the invigilator at the end of the exam.
9. Please fill in your personal details in the space provided on this page before attempting the paper.

SCIENCE OLYMPIAD FOUNDATION

Inspiring Young Minds Through Knowledge Olympiads

Name:...

SOF Olympiad Roll No.:.. Contact No.:..

1. Find the missing number, if a certain rule is followed either row-wise or column-wise.

15	18	16
30	?	21
45	40	37

A. 18 B. 20 C. 22 D. 25

2. If 'Red' means 'Yellow', 'Yellow' means 'Pink' and 'Pink' means 'Orange', then ________ is the color of Banana.

A. Yellow B. Orange
C. Red D. Pink

3. Select the combination of numbers, so that the letters are arranged accordingly to form a meaningful English word.

P E T M Y
1 2 3 4 5

A. 3, 1, 4, 2, 5 B. 2, 4, 1, 3, 5
C. 2, 1, 3, 4, 5 D. 5, 1, 4, 2, 3

4. If erasers J and U are removed from the given arrangement, then eraser ________ is fifth from the right end.

X M P J T S N U R V W (Left)

A. J B. N C. S D. U

5. Select the odd one out.

A. 

B. 

C. 

D. 

SPACE FOR ROUGH WORK

6. Which of the following keys erases the text?

A. Backspace key B. Ctrl key C. Spacebar key D. Shift key

---

7. Which of the following parts of computer keyboard allows you to quickly enter only numbers and does not contain any alphabet keys?

A. Mathematical pad B. Symbolic pad
C. Numeric keypad D. Letter pad

---

8. Which of the following input devices allows you to enter words into your computer?

A. 
B. 
C. 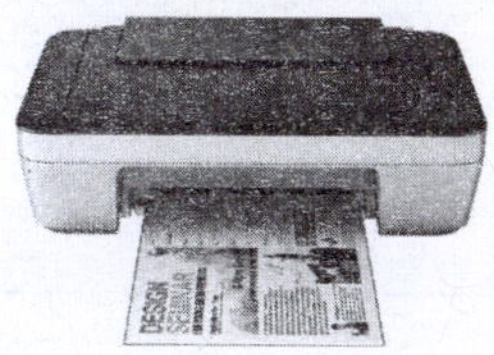
D. 

---

9. Meera is watching a movie on her computer, but she is not able to hear the voice. Help her by suggesting the CORRECT required device by unscrambling the given letters.

A. ERSEKAP B. ERTNRIP C. ERNNACS D. YOJITSCK

---

10. Which of the following storage devices comes in circular shape and requires special drive to read/write data from it?

A. Hard disk B. RAM C. Pendrive D. CD

---

11. Which of the following storage devices plugs into USB port and allows you to carry your files with you wherever you go?

A. 
B. 
C. 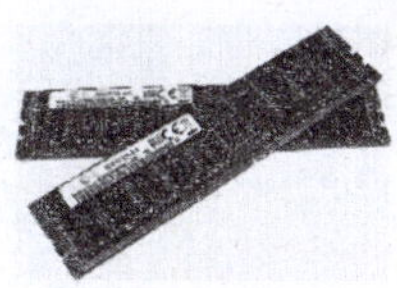
D. 

---

12. Which of the following doesn't contain RAM (Random Access Memory)?

A. 
B. 
C. 
D. 

SPACE FOR ROUGH WORK

13. The button marked as P is used to ____________ on the computer.

P

A. Move the currently opened program window from the screen temporarily to the taskbar

B. Close the currently opened program window from the screen

C. Move the currently opened program window

D. Save the currently opened program window

---

14. Identify the given image.

A. Drone

B. Throne

C. Quad

D. Smartphone

---

15. Identify the following.

- It is a handheld computer that works on a rechargeable battery.
- It has a touch sensitive screen for typing and navigation.
- It is intermediate in size between a laptop computer and a smartphone.

A. 

B. 

C. 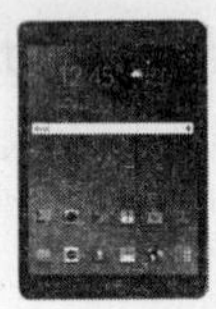

D. 

---

16. Which of the following devices can be used as an alternative of mouse?

A. 

B. 

C. 

D. 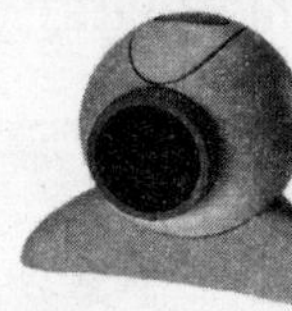

---

17. Which of the following statements is INCORRECT with respect to the uses of computer?

A. They are used to create cartoon characters in movies.

B. They cannot be used to print magazines and school books.

C. They are used to attend online classes.

D. They are used to keep the record of profit and loss in a business.

SPACE FOR ROUGH WORK

18. Each web browser contains a text box that displays the URL of the web page that is currently being viewed. This text box is known as ___________.

A. Address bar B. Textbox bar C. Name bar D. Identity bar

---

19. Which of the following areas does NOT include the use of internet?

A. Communication B. Entertainment C. Education D. Riding a bicycle

---

20. Which of the following features will be used to repeat the last performed task in MS-Word 2010?

A.  B.  C.  D. 

---

21. Which of the following tools in MS-Paint of Windows 7 is used to convert the Picture-1 into Picture-2 as shown in the given images?

A.  B. 

C.  D. 

Picture-1

Picture-2

---

22. Amit has a TV on which he can access the internet as well as play games. Which type of TV does Amit have?

A. Game TV B. Internet TV C. Smart TV D. Stereo TV

---

23. Which of the following statements is CORRECT about the storage device shown in the given picture?

A. It is a temporary storage device.
B. It stores very less amount of data.
C. It is built inside the CPU box.
D. It holds all the I/O devices together.

---

24. Given image is of a microcomputer. What do you understand by a microcomputer?

A. A small computer with a microprocessor.
B. A computer used by scientists to research about micro-technology.
C. A computer which is developed by merging two mainframe computers.
D. A computer used for robotics.

SPACE FOR ROUGH WORK

25. I am a pointing input device, commonly used to select or modify data directly on screen.

A. 
B. 
C. 
D. 

26. Which of the following options in MS-Paint of Windows 7 is accessible through View tab and helps you to align pictures properly?

A. Title bar
B. Gridlines
C. Status bar
D. Name bar

27. Which of the following statements holds true?

Statement 1 : Computers give inaccurate results.

Statement 2 : Hard disk is the main storage device found outside the CPU cabinet.

A. Only Statement 1
B. Only Statement 2
C. Both Statement 1 and Statement 2
D. Neither Statement 1 nor Statement 2

28. Arrange following steps in the CORRECT order to make an IPO cycle.

Step-1 Step-2 Step-3

A. Step-2 → Step-3 → Step-1
B. Step-1 → Step-2 → Step-3
C. Step-3 → Step-2 → Step-1
D. Step-1 → Step-3 → Step-2

29. Which of the following does NOT come under the category of 'Accessories' in Windows 7?

A. 
B. 
C. 
D. 

30. Select the INCORRECT statement.

A. An icon in computer represents a file, folder or program.
B. Start button allows user to access Start menu.
C. Windows 7 is an example of operating system.
D. You can not set size of desktop icons as medium.

SPACE FOR ROUGH WORK

31. Select the odd one out with respect to ISPs (Internet Service Providers).

(1) Jio (2) airtel (3) BSNL (4) 

A. Both (3) and (4)
B. Both (1) and (4)
C. Both (1) and (2)
D. Only (4)

---

32. Which of the following statements is CORRECT about the keyboard keys shown in the given image?

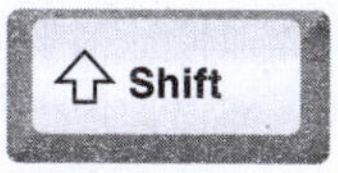

Key (1)

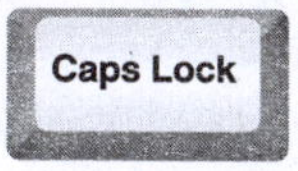

Key (2)

A. Key (1) is used to delete letters.
Key (2) is used to type capital letters continuously.

B. Key (1) is used to type one capital letter at a time.
Key (2) is used to delete letters.

C. Key (1) is used to type capital letters continuously.
Key (2) is used to type one capital letter at a time.

D. Key (1) is used to type one capital letter at a time when pressed along with any alphabet key.
Key (2) is used to type capital letters continuously.

---

33. What would be the result, if you apply the 'Flip vertical' operation on the given image in MS-Paint of Windows 7?

A. 
B. 
C. 
D. 

SPACE FOR ROUGH WORK

34. Given below are the steps required to follow if you want to cut the text from your document in MS-Word 2010:

Step-1 : Select the text you want to cut

Step-2 : Cut the selected text by pressing Ctrl + C

Step-3 : Place the cursor where you want to move the text

Step-4 : Press Ctrl + V

Select the INCORRECT step and write the correct one.

A. Step-2, Cut the selected text by pressing Ctrl + X

B. Step-4, Press Ctrl + S

C. Step-2, Cut the selected text by pressing Ctrl + Y

D. Step-2, Press Ctrl + D

---

35. Which of the following options will replace X and Y in the given diagram?

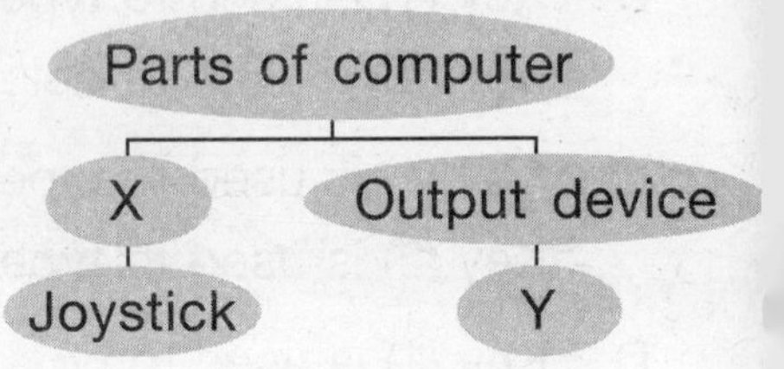

A. Input device, 

B. Storage device, 

C. Input device, 

D. Storage device, 

SPACE FOR ROUGH WORK

ANSWER KEYS

1.	(C)	**2.**	(C)	**3.**	(B)	**4.**	(C)	**5.**	(C)	**6.**	(A)	**7.**	(C)
8.	(B)	**9.**	(A)	**10.**	(D)	**11.**	(B)	**12.**	(D)	**13.**	(A)	**14.**	(A)
15.	(C)	**16.**	(B)	**17.**	(B)	**18.**	(A)	**19.**	(D)	**20.**	(B)	**21.**	(D)
22.	(C)	**23.**	(C)	**24.**	(A)	**25.**	(D)	**26.**	(B)	**27.**	(D)	**28.**	(B)
29.	(D)	**30.**	(D)	**31.**	(D)	**32.**	(D)	**33.**	(A)	**34.**	(A)	**35.**	(A)